BREAKING THE CHAINS OF COCAINE:

Black Male Addiction and Recovery

BREAKING THE CHAINS OF COCAINE:

Black Male Addiction and Recovery

Oliver J. Johnson

Cover illustration by Reginald Mackey

Photo credits:
    William Hall

    First edition, first printing

African American Images
Chicago, Illinois

DEDICATION

*This book is lovingly dedicated to
my daughter, Imani Nia Johnson.
I pray that God gives me life to witness
your fruitful marriage to a man completely
free from the chains of any addictive
disease by virtue of his walk with, and
trust in, the Lord God.*

ACKNOWLEDGEMENTS

To my wife, Valerie, thank you so much
for your encouragement. I also wish to
thank Kimberly Vann and Jawanza Kunjufu
for believing in this project. To Jawanza,
little did I know when our paths first
crossed in Chicago fourteen years
ago...isn't it amazing what God does?!

Table of Contents

Table of Contents
Continued

CHAPTER FOUR
Black Men Unshackled

Introduction

The prevention of the decimation of the African American male and the promotion of wellness activities designed to counteract these trends represent a significant challenge to public health officials, social workers, psychologists, educators, and members of the clergy. We have all heard the depressing statistics. For example, African American men continue to find themselves at the very top of the list of the six leading causes of death in the United States: homicide, heart attacks, cancer, suicide, strokes, and accidents.

Kunjufu (1990) reported that African American males are still engaged in the establishment of some truly alarming firsts: i.e., confined to special education classes, suspensions, dropouts, mental institutions, first unemployed, and denied the normal benefits of this country.

Small-Murchison (1986) reported that chemical dependency, suicide, homicide, and avoidable accidents all exhibit the escalating incidence of self-destructive patterns in the African American community and "its disproportionate share compared to society as a whole." She also asserted, "Coupled with the rising [African American] suicide and homicide rates, there is also a rise in ... [death where] an individual plays an indirect, covert, partial, or unconscious role in [his] own demise."

Indeed, can we not argue that the unpleasantness of Small-Murchison's observation does not detract from its essential truth? Can we not argue that one's own demise is created in part by the horrible devastation of cocaine dependence in the lives of African American men? In the book *Never Too Young to Die*, Peter Bell captured the essence of the crack cocaine scourge on the African American community:

"If you have cancer and I have it, how fast [the disease] will metastasize through our bodies is determined by how much either of us smoke, our diets, do we get any exercise, what's our emotional state. I think that's true with addiction, and with Black people it progresses faster."

Steadily declining life expectancy rates among African Americans represents just one of the most frightening outcomes created by the ominous presence of cocaine in our communities. According to Cole (1989):

"In its worst instances, the epidemic has even altered the biological balance of the community. Since the introduction of crack, the national rate of Black life expectancy has declined and the infant mortality rates in many Black areas have shot up."

An article in *Time Magazine* entitled "Why Do Blacks Die Young?" reported:

"The life span of both races have lengthened over the decades, but the gap between White and Black has remained stubbornly wide, and it increased sharply during the Reagan years, when many social programs that helped minorities were slashed."

These observations catapult us out of our comfort zones, cause us to critically reflect on the direction of our own lives, and create within us a renewed desire to search for concrete, practical, and workable solutions to these dilemmas. Ralph Ellison, in his riveting and timeless treasure entitled *Invisible Man*, wrote:

"I am an invisible man. No, I am not a spook like those who haunted Edgar Allen Poe; nor am I one of your Hollywood movie ectoplasms. I am a man of substance, of flesh and bone, fiber and liquids - and I might even be said to possess a mind. I am invisible, understand, simply because people refuse to see me... When they approach me they see only my surroundings, themselves, or figments of their imagination - indeed, everything and anything except me."

If we operate from the admittedly uncomfortable premise that significant numbers of African American men have some degree (perhaps, a great degree) of responsibility in their own demise, then could we not also say that we are unquestionably implicated in the process of our own demise if we choose to conform to postures of invisibility?

The very presence of the pyramids in Egypt testifies to the fact that African American men, by virtue of our own unique legacy, possess minds of extraordinary brilliance, clarity, and foresight. We have an obligation before God Almighty to relinquish the rusty shackles of invisibility. We can then become brightly visible as men created in the very image of God.

17

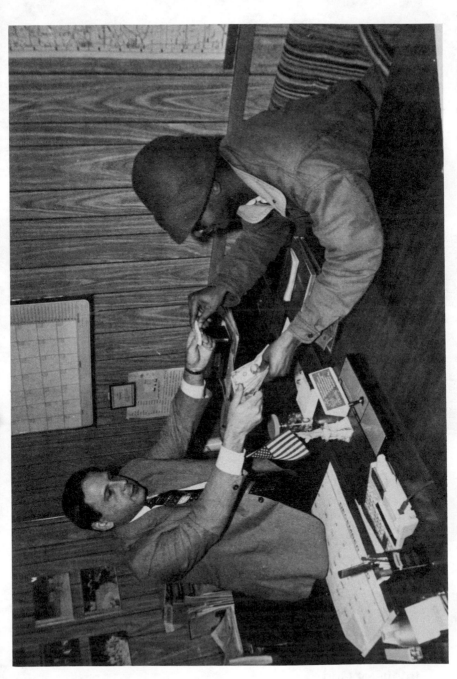

Researchers found that White males (93.4 percent) were more likely to sell drugs than Black males (67.6 percent).

The U.S. is losing the war on drugs. This pattern will continue as long as our national drug policy treats this abuse as a crime instead of a disease.

CHAPTER ONE
THE TIES THAT BIND

PROHIBITION OR LEGALIZATION

The United States had been engaged, although ambivalently at best, in an all-out assault to stop the flow of cocaine into this country, and hence, into the lives of the American people. The growth in the establishment of rehabilitative and recovery services designed to respond to the crisis of cocaine dependency has been astonishingly pronounced, dramatic, and lucrative for the chemical dependency treatment industry.

In 1988, U.S. expenditures on drug-related law enforcement activities rose to approximately ten billion dollars. At the same time, drug kingpins made about one hundred and ten billion dollars in profits. It is astonishing to note that we have consistently refused to explore the lessons of the past when it comes to previous attempts to apply criminal sanctions designed to eliminate drug abuse.

The Prohibition era of the 1920's represents a prime example. When alcohol was strictly prohibited during this period of our nation's history, criminals earned billions of dollars in profits by illegally supplying alcohol to an all too anxious public. The application of public health, instead of criminal perspectives, on the problem of drug dependency would constitute a more effective approach to this nation's "drug problem."

Baltimore mayor Kurt L. Schmoke in a 1989 interview with *Omni* Magazine boldly declared:

"It is time we brought our population of drug addicts into the public health system and out of the dark alleys, where organized crime controls the quality, quantity, and price of drugs."

Mayor Schmoke reinforces the legitimacy of his persuasive argument by further declaring in *Ebony* Magazine (August, 1989):

"The United States is losing the war on drugs, and this pattern will continue as long as our national drug policy treats drug abuse as a crime instead of a disease. Even those who strongly advocate a law enforcement approach to drugs recognize that drug-related crime is on the rise, as is the illegal importation of drugs. In Baltimore, almost 80 percent of the population of the Baltimore City Jail is incarcerated for drug-related offenses. The recent rise in drug-related arrests has simply led to more jail overcrowding without any reduction in drug use or drug-related crime.

Baltimore, like many other cities, is under court order to reduce its prison population. Building more jails will be too little, too late. Drug trafficking is so profitable and drug abuse such a serious disease, that no matter how many traffickers, pushers and users we arrest, the illegal drug trade, with all of its attendant ills, especially in our urban communities, will continue. The fact of the matter is, our current drug laws not only are not helping us win the war on drugs, they're helping us lose the war on drugs. This is true for at least three reasons.

First, we are wasting billions of dollars on law enforcement, money that could be more effectively used for education, treatment, and prevention. Second, a law enforcement approach to drugs simply raises the Black market price of drugs, making drug trafficking a progressively more attractive business for criminals. And third, because the money to be made from selling drugs is a lure to poor children, we are at risk of losing a large share of an entire generation of young people, many of whom are African American, to drug abuse, incarceration, and poverty." With respect to the question of what this nation could do to respond in a more favorable way to the problem of drugs, Mayor Schmoke asserted:

"We cannot prosecute our way out of drug abuse. The United States should put the Surgeon General in charge of the war on drugs and set up a procedure for pulling drug abusers into the public health system instead of discouraging them, with threat of prosecution, from seeking treatment.

I have recommended to Congress that a national commission be appointed to study how that strategy can best be implemented. Also, there should be enough money made available for drug abuse treatment so that any addict who seeks help can receive it on demand. And we need to consider a national needle exchange program to slow the spread of AIDS. By developing a public health strategy for the war on drugs, we will accomplish a number of important goals.

We will reduce the Black market price of drugs because these substances will be available to current users under carefully regulated medical auspices. That, in turn, will reduce drug-related crime, including the vicious turf battles that are taking so many innocent lives. Furthermore, under a public health strategy there will be more jail space available for crimes committed against persons and property, longer sentences imposed for those crimes, and less revolving door justice. Finally, a public health strategy will be a positive step toward helping the poor who, today, are bearing a disproportionate share of drug abuse, incarceration and drug-related crime. If we want to stem the drug tide, we need to treat, not prosecute those with the disease of drug addiction, and we need to educate and offer meaningful employment opportunities to millions of young Americans who are using drugs out of despair and selling drugs as a means of economic survival."

It is interesting to note that the United States began to treat drug use as a decidedly criminal offense in 1914. It is also fascinating to note the historical linkages between the country's insistence on treating drug users with criminal penalties while it simultaneously witnessed the emergence of cocaine use among African Americans and how pejorative assumptions with regard to how cocaine affected the behavior of African American men influenced criminalization decisions.

Cocaine (as we will discuss in more detail later) was thought to heighten the African American male's "innate tendencies toward uncontrollable savagery," particularly toward White women. The decision to criminalize drug use arose specifically within this context.

Beny J. Primm, in an article entitled "Drug Use: Special Implications for Black America" wrote: "Nothing is more descriptive of the attitudes of the time, and false, than a report made in 1910 by Hamilton Wright, M.D., the State Department official responsible for U.S. drug policy, in which he stated:

'The use of cocaine by negroes of the South is one of the most elusive and troublesome questions confronting the enforcement of law in most of the Southern States. Cocaine is often the direct incentive to the crime of rape by the negroes of the South and other sections of the Country.' There was never any evidence to support Wright's thesis. A study by E.M. Green, who examined 119 Blacks admitted to the Georgia State Sanitarium from 1909-1914, found only three cases of narcotic addiction among Black patients, in contrast to 142 drug-related psychoses among Whites. Of the three cases, cocaine was solely used in one instance, in combination with morphine and alcohol in another, and in combination with the opiate laudanum in the third case." Other data confirmed the low incidence of opiate use among Southern Blacks. Roberts (1885) reported the insignificant rates in North Carolina. In Tennessee, Brown (1915) found only 10 percent of the registered opiate users were Black--significantly less than their proportion in the overall population. Other reports revealed a similarly low incidence among Southern Blacks, leading these authors to conclude:

24

"The plain fact is that Dr. Wright, the chief authority of the claim of a Black cocaine problem, and later the virtual author of the Harrison Bill to ban it, was reporting unsubstantiated information and dishonestly misrepresenting the evidence available to him. Immediately after World War I, the demand for treatment for opiate use was so great that numerous narcotic clinics were started in urban areas such as New York City, Jacksonville, Florida, and New Orleans, Louisiana. In the New York City clinics, for the first time in the country, there was an overrepresentation of Black narcotic users as compared to Whites. Yet, this fact was almost totally ignored by public health officials."

African American men were thought to be in constant need of restrictive sanctions; therefore, criminal sanctions were strenuously applied. How has the misdirected decision to criminalize drug use affected the lives of African American men? In 1989, 23 percent of all African American men aged 20 to 29 were either in prison or on parole. Two-thirds of these same men were imprisoned due to drug-related offenses. The impact of male imprisonment on African American families is simply devastating. Swan (1989) accurately captures the social, economic, and psychological turbulence faced by these families:

"The crisis of imprisonment produces a double crisis for the family - demoralization and dismemberment - especially when the prisoner is a father or a husband.

Dismemberment is obvious since the family must adapt to the temporary or permanent loss of a very significant member. The absence from the family is caused by imprisonment with the probability, but not the certainty, of return by the member. In the meantime, the family must deal with the sense of shame and establishing a new relationship with the imprisoned person. This is not always necessary in some families because the absent member's input prior to imprisonment may have been such as to force many of their wives into working out a plan for their own survival. Nonetheless, during the extended period between the initial arrest and imprisonment, the wife undergoes a series of shocks: the initial arrest, the search for legal help, the search for fees, the need to secure money for bail, the loss of a job, and the expenditure of time to assure release."

A public health approach to the problem of drug abuse in the African American community would require dramatic paradigm shifts relative to how African American men are customarily perceived. In essence, we would necessarily become "real persons" in need of proactive and compassionate responses to the dilemma of addiction. The assumptions upon which rehabilitative and recovery services are based often reflect the very system of values, which upon close inspection, may actually aid in the process of explaining why so many of our African American men gravitate toward addiction's ultimately destructive journey. It can be argued that these treatment centers have neglected the clear and present need to strategically design, incorporate, and employ clinical paradigms which would unapologetically validate cultural nuances specifically unique to African American men. For example, most of the presently available treatment centers operate on the premise that drug use, in its truest essence, represents a private, individual sickness which demands a fundamental reformation of one's personal value system and self-image. Treatment is further assumed to be conducted by benign professionals with traditional values and impeccable moral standards. What this unquestionably individualistic, or linear treatment perspective fails to genuinely appreciate is the socioeconomic realities of cocaine, the values that its use reflects, and how these perspectives interface with African American men. Nobles, Goddard, Cavil, and George (1987) studied the ability of community-oriented service delivery systems to respond with effectiveness to drug-related activities on the well-being of Black children and families and found these systems to be sorely lacking.

Nobles, et. al., reported that these systems were beginning to witness behavioral, attitudinal, and psychological disturbances among service recipients that were completely foreign to them. Because of these debilitating dynamics these service delivery systems were literally unable to provide services to Black families which took the social reality of crack cocaine into account. Nobles, et. al., have also argued for a new perspective on the climate of drugs and service delivery and that these new perspectives should be understood from two distinct levels.

The first level is the environment in which recovery and rehabilitative services are provided, and the second level deals more with the actual "stuff" of treatment. Service delivery does not occur in a vacuum, nor is it divorced from the wider context of the neighborhood, community, or society. Let's examine some of the environmental influences that are quite prevalent even as one enters a treatment program with the expressed intention of breaking the terrible cycle of addiction.

ENVIRONMENTAL FORCES

Journalist Jeffery Morley, writing in *The New Republic*, captured the essence of what constitutes those factors in the environment which makes drugs so alluring:

"What if there were a drug that could chemically induce feelings of upper-middle classness?" Then he answers, "It would be a lot like crack." Our society actively cultivates, encourages, and promotes self-actualization, immediate gratification, and unabashed self-indulgence. Even the most minor pains are quickly, even casually, dismissed with pills and other aids to produce an easy lifestyle absent from struggle.

Advertising campaigns specifically targeted at African American communities attempt to delude us into thinking that smoking or drinking will make us more prestigious, smart, attractive, or popular. Research has shown that we as African Americans spend an inordinate amount of time in front of the television set. Therefore, we are disproportionately exposed to television's grandiose, yet false, and ultimately harmful message: that grave personal problems can be efficiently resolved in thirty minutes or less. All of these dynamics contribute to the presence of what Nobles, et.al., have characterized as an unmistakable "drug culture". Consequently, the provision of recovery and rehabilitation services to cocaine dependent African American men are "stuck" in an environment undeniably influenced by the prevailing drug culture. As a result, treatment outcomes become mixed at best.

A PAINFUL DILEMMA

Because of society's unrelenting emphasis on pleasurable consumption and instant gratification, cocaine is a nightmare reflecting these values. It has been demonstrated that cocaine addicts will prefer, at least initially, the known comforts of the drug and the temporary benefits it brings, to the acknowledged discomforts of "staying clean" in an environment that simply doesn't offer many other endurable or attainable pleasure.

The principles of individual and collective responsibility, humility, African American pride, sobriety and deferred gratification have very little relevance in a ravaged community whose role models for empowerment exhibit precisely the opposite traits. Therefore, cocaine addicts may appear to be quite different from the traditional stereotype of the typical drug user.

Service providers who adhere to a Westernized system of values, i.e., deferred gratification and impulse control, etc., may become quite intimidated by some of the behaviors of cocaine dependent

African American men. Nobles, et. al., have reported that service providers acknowledge feelings of ambivalence, psychic numbness, fear, disgust, and hopelessness. These feelings will necessarily serve to decrease one's effectiveness with service recipients.

New perspectives, which will be discussed at a later point in our work, are required to achieve effectiveness with cocaine dependent African American men. At the present moment however, these men are customarily relegated to the very bottom of efforts to formulate conceptual, research, and clinical treatment models designed to respond to their plight. As a result, the rapidly expanding network of chemical dependency treatment services has frequently approached cocaine dependent African American men with fear.

Significantly enough, this posture is viewed as antithetical to the start of an effective healing and recovery process. Therefore, the cocaine dependent African American male may remain transfixed in a poignant and painful dilemma as he begins his journey toward recovery. People take cocaine primarily as a way to change their brain function and to alter their moods.

The acute effects of cocaine are known to initially produce feelings of tirelessness, brilliance, spontaneity, and invulnerability. Rapidly increased energy, confidence, playfulness, sexual arousal, and mental alertness are commonly reported and have been scientifically validated. Pre-existing tensions, boredom, apathy, and fatigue may instantly vanish. Michael Davis, an African American male, shares his personal account of his experiences with cocaine in *The Family Therapy Networker:* "The crack high is not just powerful, it's overwhelming; not only elusive, but momentary, offering the kind of, "pleasure" found in dodging rush hour traffic. At its peak, the high feels like a self-induced orgasm... abruptly interrupted." Feelings of self-control and self-mastery prevail, once again, at least initially.

It is painfully ironic that it is precisely these feelings that are routinely denied African American men in their incessant quest for individual self-mastery, emotionally and spiritually fulfilling relationships and collective empowerment. Jones, et.al., (1982) reported that African American men will typically access available psychiatric and psychological treatment services when they are wrestling with depression and work-related problems. Davis and Watson, (1985) share the following incident in *Black Life in Corporate America: Swimming in the Mainstream:*

"What happens when the Black manager bumps his or her head against the relatively low ceilings? It's certain that this adds additional stress to an already stress-filled life. Since Black people have been more accustomed to handling stress, many Black managers do not speak up about their frustrations. They do not want to feel like complainers and they perceive that Whites do not really want to hear their complaints. This is illustrated by a second story told to us by a middle-level White manager in Denver about a Black co-worker. 'I had no idea that Ray was having serious problems. He was always joking and happy. I used to go out drinking with him and we used to talk about things, but I didn't think about them as deeply as he must have. I guess when it's not happening to you, you tend not to dwell on it, and I'm sure if he had dwelled on negative things I would not have wanted to keep going out drinking with him. That's why I was very surprised when he went home from work one Friday, pulled all the phones out of the wall and blew his brains out. What had happened to Ray is that he had worked extremely hard for a promotion. He had already been passed over three times and so he was three steps behind many of his contemporaries. He was bright and everyone in the district thought that he was finally going to get his promotion.

The Monday before he killed himself his boss had called him in and apologetically told him that the company had decided to promote someone else. The someone was a White male whom he had trained. This was the second time that this had happened. He freaked out'."

More frequent instances of the micro-aggressions that we as African American men face on a daily basis in the workplace is recorded here by Davis and Watson:

"Another Black manager said, 'I had a manager once who would ask every one of my White peers the answer to a certain question, and it would never occur to him to ask me. He simply assumed that I didn't know. I remember once he wanted to know the capital of Burma. So he asked everyone around me. No one knew. He called his wife at home and got her to look it up in a set of encyclopedias. She came back with the answer Mandalay. He put that name in the report he was writing. At first, I decided to let it go and then I changed my mind. I went up to his desk, reached over his shoulder and crossed out Mandalay and wrote Rangoon just above it. I told him that Rangoon is the capital. He looked up surprised and asked, "Why didn't you tell us, Louis?" I said, 'You didn't ask me. You asked the person to the left of me then you skipped over me and asked the person to the right of me.' I asked him if he noticed that he had asked everyone in the section except me, and it never occurred to him that since I was fresh out of the Vietnam War and had been in Southeast Asia, I should have been the one he asked first'."

Interestingly enough, Gary and Berry (1985) conducted a study to determine the incidence and prevalence of depressive symptoms among African American men. They discovered that the most significant predictor of depression for African American men was conflict between Black men and Black women. Na'im Akbar (1989) provides us with an eloquent description of some of the pivotal causes for this conflict. He also provides us with some innovative paradigm shifts which could help us to rebuild and stabilize our relationships:

"The economic insolvency of the African American man, the exploitation of the African American woman, the disproportionate numbers of African American men victimized by the penal system , the continued absence of effective political control and general control over the destiny of

33

our communities continue to undermine the stability of male/female relationships. In the final analysis, the reconciliation of the African American woman and man is a philosophical reconciliation. An exorcism of the deeply embedded false premises regarding materialism and sexism must occur in our thinking. We must rediscover the ancient definitions of man and woman and respect their differences and their complementarity. Ancient writers who found the origin of their wisdom on the African continent have long ago asserted that the true identity of man and woman is an inner identity. These writers suggest that we can find the prototype of the man's function in his basic role as father. Similarly, the prototype of the woman's function is the role of mother. These ancient definitions, of course, attributed a much broader meaning to motherhood and fatherhood than the biological definitions of these roles. Fatherhood was viewed as a societal function which went far beyond a male's capacity to sire offspring. True manhood was identified in the human qualities of personal mastery and rational direction which equipped man to be a provider and protector of society. Motherhood was viewed as a nurturing societal function. In whatever role the woman found herself, her obligation was to nourish, cultivate, inspire and facilitate societal and human growth. Such qualities focus the developing person on her or his inner self. In order to serve these functions, the physical characteristics, material possessions, sexual roles and functions all become secondary and incidental to the bigger definition of self. African American men and women must not fall victim to the expanding unisexualism so prevalent in American society. They must preserve the uniqueness of their separate, complementary roles. They must also avoid the ontological weakness which equates nurturing, dependence and supportiveness with weakness. They must also avoid the highly destructive macho notions of manhood which are feverishly trying to be realized by both men and women in their striving for a faulty liberation. We must avoid the growing individualistic mania which avows a false independence of men and women."

If left unattended, these issues will negatively impinge upon one's ability to establish mutually productive and fulfilling relationships at home.

Any discussion of cocaine dependency among African American men would be incomplete without some reverent examination of the Honorable Elijah Muhammad's program of salvaging these men (including his chief disciple, Malcolm X) from the ravages of drug addiction. The Honorable Elijah Muhammad's program provides us with an excellent example of how an intimate appreciation of who we are as African American men helps us to transcend the peculiarly oppressive obstacles of cocaine addiction. The Honorable Elijah Muhammad's program was unparalleled for its astonishing ability to rehabilitate dispossessed and disenfranchised men. A number of these men were "hopelessly" dependent upon drugs prior to their introduction to the teachings of this amazing man. The Honorable Elijah Muhammad's teaching also successfully eliminated other types of unhealthy habits, i.e., liquor consumption, nicotine dependence, and sugar and pork consumption.

How did his program accomplish its objectives for the rebirth of African American men? The Honorable Elijah Muhammad was resolutely determined to define himself in accordance with the powerful and inspiring truths of who we were as African American men many thousands of years ago.

Akbar (1991) describes the sense of resolve that served as the foundation for the Honorable Elijah Muhammad's task:

> "Such determination to define oneself is the kind of characteristic that typifies Elijah Muhammad and the work he did. He demanded that in order to empower self you must first know yourself. 'Knowledge of self, he said, is the key to power.' This is a Black man talking to Black men and Black women and Black children. To the Black world, he said self-knowledge is the key. Little did we know that this man had reached all the way back beneath the pyramids, down through the temples of Karnak, looked through the documents of old and found the message written in the hieroglyphs, going back over five thousand years that said, 'Man, know thyself.'"

Malcolm X deserves special mention as well. Malcolm stepped into the transforming context of the Honorable Elijah Muhammad's program of self-renewal and into the annals of history as one of the most influential figures of our time. He is an increasingly popular figure among our youth, having evolved from the life of Malcolm Little, to the life of Detroit Red, to the life of Malcolm X, to the short life and death of El-Hajj Malik El Shabazz.

As a result of the evolutionary process that Malcolm X went through, the depth of his spirit was fundamentally indomitable, compelling, brilliant and so very engaging. By letters and visits from his family, Malcolm was awakened to the truths of the Honorable Elijah Muhammad's teachings after his arrest and conviction on burglary charges in 1946. In prison, he formulated his own program of self-education.

Upon his release from prison at the age of 27 in 1952, he came under the personal tutelage of the Honorable Elijah Muhammad and became the Nation of Islam's most outstanding spokesman. He withdrew from the Nation of Islam in 1964 and founded the Organization of Afro-American Unity. His pilgrimage to Mecca in 1964 led him to embrace the true roots of his Islamic faith.

Tragically, Malcolm was assassinated in Harlem, New York on February 21, 1965. Ossie Davis delivered an impeccably resplendent eulogy at Malcolm's funeral. We have captured the essence of Mr. Davis' stirring message here:

"Many will ask what Harlem finds to honor in this stormy, controversial and bold young captain - and we will smile. Many will say turn away - away from this man, for he is not a man but a demon, a monster, a subverter and an enemy of the Black man - and we will smile. They will say that he is of hate - a fanatic, a racist - who can only bring evil to the cause for which you struggle! And we will answer and say unto them: Did you ever talk to Brother Malcolm? Did you ever touch him, or have him smile at you? Did you ever really listen to him? Did he ever do a mean thing? Was he himself ever associated with violence or any public disturbance? For if you did, you would know him. And if you knew him, you would know why we must honor him; Malcolm was our manhood, our living, Black manhood! This was his meaning to his people. And in honoring him, we honor the best in ourselves. Last year, from Africa, he wrote these words to a friend: 'My journey,' he says, 'is almost ended, and I have a much broader scope than when I started out, which I believe will add new life and dimension to our struggle for freedom and honor and dignity in the States. I am writing these things so that you will know for a fact the tremendous sympathy and support we have among the African States for our Human Rights struggle. The main thing is that we keep a united front wherein our most valuable time and energy will not be wasted fighting each other.' "However much we may have differed with him - or with each other about him and his value as a man - let his going from us serve only to bring us together, now. Consigning these mortal remains to earth, the common mother of all, should be secure in the knowledge that what we place in the ground is no more now a man - but a seed - which, after the winter of our discontent, will come forth again to meet us. And we will know him then for what he was and is - a Prince - our own Black shining Prince! - who didn't hesitate to die, because he loved us so."

Malcolm broke free from the burdens of his addictions because he courageously embraced his legacy as a strong warrior.

The probable existence of a "shame-based core" resident with cocaine dependent African American men merits special attention. One of the central characteristics of persons with this inward wound is that they are unquestionably defective in some irredeemable way. To be more specific, a shame-based core is fundamentally rooted on the mistaken premise that one is defective not because of some lack of accomplishment; more importantly, persons with a shame-based core hold tenaciously to a belief that they are defective simply because of who they are.

Whitfield (1989) has observed that a shame-based core originates from the negative messages, beliefs, rules, and affirmations which we invariably internalize as we grow up. Whitfield has also presented a list (which we have condensed) of some of the more common rules and messages. As you review this abbreviated list, we ask that you would pay special attention to those indicators which seem to be particularly relevant to what we typically hear in African American families, i.e., "Be a man," "Don't discuss the family with outsiders."

NEGATIVE RULES
Don't express your feelings
Don't get angry
Don't get upset
Don't cry
Do as I say, not as I do
Be good, "nice", perfect
Avoid conflict (or avoid dealing with conflict)
Don't think or talk; just follow directions
Do well in school
Don't ask questions

Don't betray the family
Don't discuss the family with outsiders
Be seen and not heard
No back talk
Don't contradict me
Always look good
I'm always right; you're always wrong
Always be in control

NEGATIVE MESSAGES

Shame on you
You're not good enough
I wish I'd never had you
Your needs are not alright with me
Hurry up and grow up
Be dependent
Be a man
Big boys don't cry
You don't feel that way
Don't be like that
You're so stupid
You caused it
You owe it to us
Of course we love you!
I'm sacrificing myself for you
How can you do this to me?
We won't love you if you...
You're driving me crazy
You'll never accomplish anything

It is also important to note that a shame-based core can emerge as part of our exposure to institutional arrangements within the larger society that consistently projects unhealthy images about our capabilities of African American men. Parents who are about the business of "unintentionally" belittling the God-given personhood and talents of African American boys are laying the foundation for the development of a shame-based core which will emerge at a later juncture in their lives.

Examples include:

Kenneth is ashamed and feeling inadequate as a result of being severely mistreated as a boy. He has "inexplicable" periods of becoming enraged at his own children. He begins to use drugs to drown out his emotional pain.

Sam was constantly ridiculed by his brothers at home for "being Blacker than the rest of us." His mother did nothing to prevent their cruelty. Sam now feels that he must avoid African American businesses at all costs because, "they all treat you like dirt."

The presence of a shame-based core becomes intolerable; therefore, both of these men are prime candidates for the development of an addictive disorder because the addiction serves to mask the inward pain.

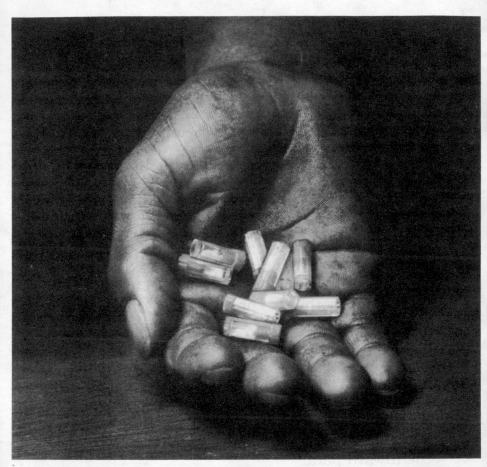

Yo, slave!

**This dealer is selling something you don't want.
You'll pay more than just cash money.
You'll trade in your hopes, your dreams....
even your self-respect.**

Now, do you really want to buy?

Addiction is slavery.

CHAPTER TWO
BLACK MEN IN
BONDAGE

THE CYCLE OF COCAINE DEPENDENCY

The cocaine high is extraordinarily pleasurable but extremely brief. Then, the unimaginable begins to happen, sometimes instantaneously: The cocaine dependent person will aggressively pursue that same fleeting high as their number one priority. Gradually, a predictable pattern begins to emerge. This pattern tends to progress through the following stages (May, 1988):

denial and suppression
rationalization
cover up
stalling strategies
surrender
exaltation
brokenness

DENIAL AND SUPPRESSION

In the early stages of cocaine dependence, our minds will strenuously downplay all indications of increasing reliance upon the drug. We will avoid moments of quiet reflection and restfulness because it is precisely during those times that the true horrors of what our addiction has done to us comes crashing to the surface of our conscious minds - thereby shattering our sense of false peace, serenity, and equilibrium.

Frank was an example. He was introduced to crack cocaine during a party that he had attended after work. He quickly became entangled in the web of addiction. Yet, he would persistently deny its reality. He began to pawn his wife's possessions, withdrew money that he had set aside for his son's college education, and embezzled money from work.

When confronted with his behavior, he would become indignant and deny what the addiction was doing to his values system.

RATIONALIZATION

Here is where the cycle becomes subtly, yet irrefutably vicious. Excuses are used in an effort to justify the presence of the addiction; "I smoke crack because we brothers need something to make ourselves feel stronger." Rationalizations, of course, can have deadly consequences. Len Bias reportedly celebrated his selection as the first round draft pick of the Boston Celtics in 1986 by smoking cocaine. A cocaine-induced cardiac arrest reportedly killed him. To us, Len's death stands unchallenged as the saddest sports story of the 1980's. Stories like the one John A. Martin cites in *Blessed Are The Addicts; The Spiritual Side of Alcoholism, Addiction, and Recovery* (1989) are not uncommon:

44

"Before he began to use drugs, Ramon lived with his wife and two children aged five and three in New York City. The family was on welfare and lived in a run-down neighborhood, and life was not happy. His relationship with his wife was strained, and he was beginning to physically abuse his children. Ramon himself was unconsciously bored, lonely, and depressed.

In his mind, a job, if he could find one, would give him a renewed purpose, self-esteem, and hope of improving his family's living conditions. He was certain that the job was the "key" that would finally open up his life to the realization of all his dreams. Suddenly, he had a job, and for a while Ramon felt centered. He was proud of himself again. He had found the answer, and nothing, so it seemed to him, could go wrong. He had even saved a down payment for a second-hand car. But the feeling of discontent, the burden of daily living, slowly returned. Once again, things seemed to be getting out of control. He couldn't seem to hang on to life once he thought he had it in the palm of his hand. At this point, he was introduced to drugs. Co-workers enticed him to try some crack. Within six months, this devastating drug started him on the road of truly believing, once again, that he was in charge of his destiny. Overnight, Ramon abandoned his car at JFK Airport without telling anyone, not even his family or his employer, flew to a remote village in Puerto Rico, and lived with his mother. Sure that in a radical change of place and lifestyle he would rediscover the happy life, within a month of his move he contacted his wife, instructed her to pack their belongings, prepare the two boys, and move down to the island with him. The hesitancy in her voice at the prospect of making such a radical move prompted Ramon to convince her at length of how things would be great for all of them. Finally, she went. What awaited Ramon's family in Puerto Rico can only be described as sheer disaster. By this time, Ramon was heavily into drugs and debt. He was jobless and his mother had evicted him from her house. At last word, the wife and children were staying with Ramon's mother while looking for the necessary money to return to New York City. As for Ramon, they hadn't seen him recently and even feared for his life. From Ramon's long search for a solution to life - before the use of drugs - he had reached the point of once again believing in the possibility of fixing his life through the proper maneuver of external circumstances and situations - this time under the influence of the drug, or if you will, of the full-blown disease of addiction. But his effort to "fix", to control things, only led to greater disaster for himself and his loved ones."

Other examples of rationalizations include: "I can stop my use of cocaine at any time;" "I'm married. I have a nice job, so what if I happen to do a little cocaine on the side;" "I have never been busted, so it's no problem for me."

COVER UP

At this stage, denial, suppression, and rationalization assume some truly depressing dimensions. These defense mechanisms are unfortunately still working too well, but the truth of the sheer magnitude of one's dependence upon cocaine cannot be contained. Cocaine dependent African American men may try desperately to project images of success, competence, or what Majors and Billson (1992) define as a style of behavior which would necessarily prevent one's attempts at recovery; the "Cool Pose". They assert: "Cool pose is a distinctive coping mechanism that serves to counter, at least in part, the dangers that Black males encounter on a daily basis. As a performance, cool pose is designed to render the Black male visible and to empower him; it eases the worry and pain of blocked opportunities. Being cool is an ego booster for Black males comparable to the kind White males more easily find through attending good schools, landing prestigious jobs, and bringing home decent wages. Cool pose is constructed from attitudes and actions that become firmly entrenched in the Black male's psyche as he adopts a facade to ward off the anxiety of second-class status. It provides a mask that suggests competence, high self-esteem, control, and inner strength. It also hides doubt, insecurity, and inner turmoil. By acting calm, emotionless, fearless, aloof, and tough, the African American male strives to offset an externally imposed "zero" image. Being cool shows both the dominant culture and the Black male himself that he is strong and proud. He is somebody. He is a survivor, in spite of the systematic harm done by the legacy of slavery and the realities of racial oppression, in spite of centuries of hardship and mistrust."

Similarly, Whitfield (1987) describes a "persona" with a number of fascinating parallels to the mask so synonymous with the tendency to conceal our true selves. He writes: "Most of the time, in the role of our false, or co-dependent self, we feel uncomfortable, numb, empty, or in a contrived state. We do not feel real, complete, whole or sane. At one level or another, we sense that something is wrong, something is missing. Paradoxically, we often feel like this false self is our natural state, the way we "should be." This could be our addiction or attachment to being that way. We become so accustomed to being our co-dependent self that our Real Self feels guilty, like something is wrong, that we shouldn't feel real or alive. To consider changing this problem is frightening."

Whitfield also quotes Charles Finn's accurate description of the turmoil involved with our attempts to hide our true selves:

PLEASE HEAR WHAT I'M NOT SAYING

Don't be fooled by me.
Don't be fooled by the face that I wear.
For I wear a mask, a thousand masks,
    masks that I'm afraid is me.
Pretending is an art that's second nature with me,
    but don't be fooled.
For God's sake don't be fooled.
I give you the impression that I'm secure,
    that all is sunny and unruffled with me,
        within as well as without,
        that confidence is my name
        and coolness my game,
    that the water's calm and I'm in command,
        and that I need no one.
But don't believe me.
My surface may seem smooth but my
        surface is my mask,
    ever varying and ever concealing.

Beneath lies no complacence.
Beneath lies confusion and fear and aloneness,
but I hide this. I don't want anybody to know it.

I panic at the thought of my weakness
and fear being exposed.
That's why I frantically create a mask
to hide behind,
a nonchalant sophisticated facade,
to help me pretend,
to shield me from the glance that knows.
But such a glance is precisely my salvation.
My only hope and I know it.
That is, if it's followed by acceptance,
if it's followed by love,
it's the only thing that can liberate me
from myself,
from my own self-built prison walls,
from the barriers I so painstakingly erect.
It's the only thing that will assure me of what I
can't assure myself,
that I'm really worth something.
But I don't tell you this. I don't dare. I'm afraid to.
I'm afraid your glance will not be
followed by acceptance,
will not be followed by love.
I'm afraid you'll think less of me, that you'll laugh,
and your laugh would kill me.
I'm afraid that deep-down I'm nothing,
that I'm just no good,
and that you will see this and reject me.
So I play my game,
my desperate pretending game,
with a facade of assurance without
and a trembling child within.
So begins the glittering but empty
parade of masks,

and my life becomes a front.
I idly chatter to you in the same suave tones of
surface talk.
I tell you everything that's really nothing,
and nothing of what's everything
and what's crying within me.
So when I'm going through my routine,
do not be fooled by what I'm saying.
Please listen carefully and try to hear
what I'm not saying,
what I'd like to able to say,
what for survival I need to say,
but what I can't say.
I don't like to hide.
I don't like to play superficial phony games.
I want to stop playing them.
I want to be genuine and spontaneous and me,
but you've got to help me.
You've got to hold out your hand
even when that's the last thing I seem to want.
Only you can wipe away from my eyes the
blank stare of the
breathing dead.
Only you can call me into aliveness.
Each time you're kind and gentle
and encouraging,
each time you try to understand because you
really care,
my heart begins to grow wings,
very small wings,
very feeble wings,
but wings!
With your power to touch me into feeling
you can breathe life into me.
I want you to know that.
I want you to know how important you are to me,
how you can be a creator -
an honest-to-God creator -

50

of the person that is me
if you choose to.
You alone can break down the wall
behind which I tremble,
you alone can remove my mask,
you alone can release me from my shadow-world of
panic and uncertainty,
from my lonely prison,
if you choose to.
Please choose to. Do not pass me by.
It will not be easy for you.
A long conviction of worthlessness builds
strong walls.
The nearer you approach to me,
the blinder I may strike back.
It's irrational, but despite what the books
say about man,
often I am irrational.
I fight against the very thing that I cry out for.
But I am told that love is stronger
than strong walls,
and in this lies my hope,
Please try to beat down those walls
with firm hands
but with gentle hands
for a child is very sensitive.

Who am I, you may wonder?
I am someone you know very well.
For I am every man you meet
and I am every woman you meet.

And of course, Paul Laurence Dunbar brilliantly penned one of the most timeless illustrations of the pain involved and the need to "cover
up" as an African American male in "We Wear
the Mask", in 1906:

WE WEAR THE MASK

We wear the mask that grins and lies,
It hides our cheeks and shades our eyes,
This debt we pay to human guile;
With torn and bleeding hearts we smile,
And mouth myriad subtleties.

Why should the world be otherwise,
In counting all our tears and sigh?
Nay, let them only see us, while
we wear the mask.

We smile, but, O great Christ, our cries,
To thee from tortured souls arise.
We sing, but oh, the clay is vile,
Beneath our feet, and long the mile;
But let the world dream otherwise,
We wear the mask!

STALLING STRATEGIES

In this stage, cocaine dependent African American men may subscribe to a set of beliefs which, on the surface, sound perfectly reasonable and rational; "I realize that cocaine is enslaving me. But, I'm not a slave to anyone or anything. I'll emancipate myself from the shackles of this deadly substance in my own time." However, we still haven't truly surrendered. We may think, "I'll quit after I take that last hit with the fellas."

Again, Martin (1990) cites a case which is all too poignant when we consider the remarkable degree to which addicts will procrastinate:

"Ellen, from the Midwest, was brought up to be ambitious, industrious, and serious about her goals. She wanted to be an architect, but life for Ellen wasn't all work and no play. During her college years, she learned how to smoke pot and drink margaritas as well if not better than the rest of them. A few mishaps occurred. She was involved in two minor car accidents, and had gotten herself in a situation that resulted in an abortion - all of this as a direct result of her excessive use and abuse of alcohol and drugs. Fortunately, she finished her college course seemingly unscathed. Her parents were unaware of her questionable escapades, and the difficulties the drugs had put her in were all somehow ironed out with no embarrassing consequences. Most importantly, her future plans were clear. She would move to New York City, enroll at Pratt Institute, and land an entry-level job in her field. Naturally, she would share an apartment, since her funds would continue at the outset to be sparse.

Poor Ellen never got to the Registrar's Office, nor did she even search for an entry-level position. She did find an apartment. Unfortunately, it was a "share" with a girl whose boyfriend not only dealt drugs, but used the apartment to ply his trade. During her very first week in the city, Ellen decided to postpone acting on her plans for one month. She would give herself one month to "adjust" as she put it, to her new environment. At the end of that month, she was so well-adjusted that not only was she progressing in her addiction, selling her body on orders of the boyfriend to the customers who passed through day and night, but considered her original plans to make no sense.

53

In Ellen's case, the first stages of physical addiction took her life solidly and progressed rapidly. In one week's time, she decided to postpone her plan of action for one month. Within a short month, she had put it off for at least a year. It's been five years since that time. I am sad to report that Ellen is not better. She presently lives in a crack house. She appears gaunt and hopeless. She has aged beyond her years. When I would, on occasion, meet her on the street, she would tell me, 'I'm rethinking my goals. I still want to go to Pratt. And I will, maybe next year. For now, though, there are many things that I need to do.' The sad truth is that Ellen has nothing to do. She has lost her ability to choose. She has to continue to use."

SURRENDER

This stage is really representative of a false surrender to the self, not a liberating surrender to the healing power of God's grace. In pseudo-surrender, the cocaine dependent African American male may become so depressed over repeated failures to break his addiction that he just simply gives in to it. Remorse, shame, and guilt are palpable by-products of this stage.

Calvin said that he had stopped using cocaine, "completely on my own. I didn't need any help from God or any other so-called Higher Power. It didn't take me that long either. That bull about the pain involved in giving up cocaine is a tired myth. Now, I'm going to help other brothers break their addictions."

Calvin underestimated his potential for relapse. He returned to his use of cocaine after becoming depressed over his bank's refusal to refinance his home.

EXALTATION

This stage is absolutely demonic in its ability to deceive. The natural sense of satisfaction at having abstained from cocaine will be subtly replaced by pride. With the onset of pride, the descent back into the eventual use of cocaine begins. Self-exaltation means that we have neglected to attribute our abstinence to God. Instead, we start to believe, "I did it. It was really no big deal. I knew that my own intelligence, resolve, and perseverance could conquer this crazy little addiction!" Whenever and in whatever form self-exaltation occurs, a fall back into cocaine use is only a matter of time.

Again, Martin (1990) cogently summarizes the primary issues integral to this stage:

> "At this point, the lie begins. The spirit is not properly identified. What the addict thinks is his human spirit, finally freed and able to breathe and function as he always wanted it to, is merely the short-lived effects of the drug. The American Indians, upon discovering alcohol, deftly labeled it a 'spirit.'
>
> The pain prior to the drug is an unending sign of the human spirit toward life and living, and the discovery of the drug is mistakenly identified as the realization of that goal. At this point, the drug in reality doesn't work because it makes the addict believe he is who he is not and believe he is not who he is. The addict genuinely thinks that his renewed zest for life is rooted in the real "him." This is the beginning of the lie, of

the tragedy that spawns so much future pain for the drug addict. This renewed hope in life is rooted not in the human spirit but in a chemical that has no spiritual or human reality. And the addict very quickly (almost immediately) recognizes this."

BROKENNESS

Here is where every measure of one's dignity and worth vanishes. Any remaining remnants of one's capacity to withstand further usage of cocaine evaporates, and one's use of the drug becomes blatantly pronounced, embittered, and severe. Still, even in the horrible midst of this stage, prideful elements of the self continue to be pathetically exerted. In this stage, (which, if left unchecked will surely result in premature death) cocaine use may actually accelerate.

Again, Michael Davis says, "The sensation seldom lasts a minute; then, all hell breaks loose for the rest of the day. The street phrase for this hellishness is 'chasing the rock.' Thus, the two components of the crack high: the peak and the chase. What begins as orgasm soon becomes trickery. The thrills and chills are replaced by primal screams. Where a natural orgasm is ushered out by a resolved feeling, crack breaks its climax at peak, leaving the user hanging, ripe for the chase. But each subsequent hit delivers less peak and more hook until that "sneaking desire" Morley describes becomes like a pit-bull in slippers. The user buys another rock and another. It's not uncommon to see users in a frenzy, on their hands and knees, pathetically searching for imaginary lost crumbs of crack."

In a sad and misdirected attempt to maintain the intense feelings of ecstasy, the cocaine dependent African American male will begin to take more and more doses of cocaine at progressively and frighteningly shorter intervals. Laboratory animals will take cocaine to the point of exhaustion or death. These animals will choose cocaine over water, food, and sex. They will willingly put up with excruciatingly painful electrical shocks - all for the opportunity to consume increasingly larger amounts of cocaine.

These experiments are undeniably illustrative of cocaine's demonic power to enslave and destroy African American men. He doesn't have to come from a single-parent home, be underemployed, or unemployed to succumb to cocaine's astonishing power to unmercifully dismantle him. A "cocaine crash" follows as quickly as the high subsides. This state, which is characterized by feelings of depression, misery, and worthlessness, becomes literally intolerable.

The user may tragically believe that he can eliminate these decidedly unpleasant moods by simply taking more cocaine. However, more cocaine gradually produces feelings of anxiety, restlessness, agitation, irritability, and insomnia. Continued use leads to confusion, hypervigilence, suspiciousness, and paranoid delusions. Michael Davis describes his descent with graphic detail:

"But the most horrifying tendency of this drug is what it makes the user do, especially after the last rock and dollar are gone. I saw it in myself and everyone else using or selling. It stirs up a self-centered trance that locks us into our most primitive responses. Crack made lying, stealing, adultery, meanness, and violence all too easy. Crack enters the brain's most intimate room, then proceeds with psychological, emotional, physical, spiritual, financial, and social rape. It's born of a lie - 'This is an orgasm, let's do it again' - then is fed by other lies."

Hence, the psychopharmacological effects of cocaine provide African American men with a powerful substitute for feelings.

Living in a culture that tends to promote personal wellness and the development of addictive behaviors intended to maximize the same leads to the following set of questions: Can African American men sustain a sense of self-worth without drugs? Must he become sedated in order to elevate himself to a position of self-affirmation and empowerment? Must we always mask our real longing for God with all sorts of superficial "items" e.g., insatiable achievement, acquisitions, the incessant pursuit of material and sensual pleasures, etc., in order to reclaim our legacy and heritage as strong African American men?

In an extraordinarily gentle and engaging manner, Gerald May (1991) beautifully describes our dilemma in his work entitled: *The Awakened Heart: Living Beyond Addiction.* May declares that our tendencies toward addictions of various kinds, i.e., work, sex, drugs, gambling, etc., are actually

58

futile manifestations of our desire to escape an inner sense of emptiness that only God can truly fulfill.

We mistakenly assume that we can fulfill ourselves and that if we can't, something is awfully wrong with us. In order to capture the essence of May's provocative message, we have taken the liberty of presenting a significant portion of his work on the fallacy of our attempts to find fulfillment in the midst of our addictions. He writes:

"We would rather have the anesthetized serenity of dullness than the liberating disease of truth. Together, our addiction to fulfillment and our flight from truth weave a harsh, desperate barrier against participation in love. Back in the days when I was doing a lot of psychotherapy, a Roman Catholic priest came to me with this concern: 'I'm nearly fifty years old, and I still don't have my sexuality resolved.' My response, perhaps a bit too flippant, was, "Join the crowd." 'No,' he said, 'I mean it. I'm not satisfied with my relationships and I can't make peace with celibacy. I can't find any serenity with my desire for intimacy. 'I still felt it sounded quite normal, but he wanted to work on it. So for several months, we explored whether psychological problems were causing his distress. He had not received perfect love and support from his parents when he was a child, but I thought, "Who does?" He had been traumatized in a variety of ways by early sex education and experiences. I wondered, "Aren't we all, to some degree?" I couldn't escape my conviction that he was a very normal example of the male human species. A middle-aged mother told a story not unlike that of the priest. 'I should be happy with the way things are. I have a fine marriage, two wonderful kids, a good career. Yet I keep feeling something is missing. I have these dreams about romance. Deep down I am restless; I want something more. I think my sex life is as good as the next person's, but there's some kind of intimacy I long for. I think perhaps I am repressing something.' I asked, "Is there any particular reason you feel this is a problem? Could it be that many other people have similar yearnings for something more? (This was my attempt at a gentler version of 'Join the crowd.')" She paused for a long time then continued, 'No, I do not believe other people have these feelings. I know a lot of people who are perfectly happy and fulfilled.' I replied, "Do you think they really are or is it maybe just the way they act and talk? I know I hear this kind of thing from many people." She responded, 'Well, you talk to a lot of strange people. I have some close friends who never seem to feel the way I do. If they're kidding themselves, they're doing a good job of it. They feel really contented with their lives.' I asked her, "Have you ever talked to them? Have you told any of them how you feel, to see what they'd say? She replied, 'No, I haven't. They wouldn't understand. And I'd feel - I do feel - as though there's something wrong with me. They'd give me advice and that's the last thing I need. I already feel too incapable.' So we explored her psychology for a while. As with the priest, there were imperfections, but again I kept thinking that all experience is imperfect. And I keep wanting to say, "What's wrong with feeling unfulfilled and restless? Isn't there something basically right about it?" With both of these people, as with so many others who have confided in me, the real problem was believing that their sense of inner restlessness and lack of fulfillment indicated psychological disorder. They swallowed the cultural myth that says, 'If you are well-adjusted, and if you are living your life properly, you will feel fulfilled, satisfied, content and serene.' Stated conversely, the myth says, 'If you are not satisfied and fulfilled, there is something wrong with you.' The myth is so widespread that the majority of adults in our culture accept it without question. There are three ways we act out this belief. We may try to "fix" ourselves, our life situations, and our relationships because we feel something is wrong with them. Or we may repress our restlessness, trying to appear to ourselves and others as if we had achieved perfection. Failing this, we dull our concern altogether, seeking to lose ourselves in work, food, entertainment, drugs, or some other escape. Ironically, all three ways easily become addictions themselves: addictions to self-improvement, to perfect adjustment, or to various means of escape. The myth has pervaded virtually every aspect of our society. Popular religion promises peace of mind if only we believe correctly. If we are not completely happy, it maintains, it is because we are somehow not right with God. Perhaps we are too sinful, or our faith is insufficient, or we have missed the one true doctrine. Countless people believe the religious myth, even when a cursory reading of the lives of saints reveals great agony, doubt, and struggle within themselves and with their world. A slightly deeper probing of spiritual growth shows that as people deepen in their love for God and others, they become ever more open - not only more appreciative of the beauty and joys of life, but also more vulnerable to its pain and brokenness. Popular psychology promotes the myth as well. It promises peace of mind for only two categories of people: those who grew up in perfectly functioning families and those who use modern psycholgy to rise above the scars of their dysfunctional families. Countless people believe this psychological version as well, even when the knotted lives of our most successful citizens are continually displayed in the media for all to examine and when no such thing as a truly functional family can be found. Although it is very right to treat our real disorders and maximize our health, we make several great mistakes if we think life should or even can be resolved to a point of complete serenity and fulfillment. To believe this is to commit ourselves to a fantasy that does not exist and that, if it were true, would kill our love and end in stagnation, boredom, and death. It is also to remove our energy to a vague, self-serving agenda that must be carried out before we can get on with the business of living, loving, and creating a better world. Further, the myth perpetuates the willful delusion that we human beings are objects and like objects or machines, to be built and repaired, designed for efficiency rather than love. Most importantly, the myth of fulfillment makes us miss the most beautiful aspects of our human souls: our emptiness, our incompleteness, our radical yearning for love. We were never meant to be completely fulfilled; we were meant to taste it, to long for it, and to grow toward it. In this way we participate in love becoming life, life becoming love. To miss our emptiness is, finally, to miss our hope."

As the Director of the Pastoral Counseling Center at Greenforest Baptist Church, I too have come to believe that our desires for fulfillment will never be completely realized during our sojourn on this earth. Instead, we will find true rest only when we consciously decide to rest in God. As Gerald May asserts in another of his works entitled *Addiction and Grace: Love and Spirituality in the Healing of Addiction* "Addictions, then, displaces and supplants God's love as the source and object of our deepest true desire." African American men may, at first, inadvertently establish an enduring relationship with cocaine to compensate for the emotional vacuum created by the vicissitudes to which he is subjected to on increasingly ominous dimensions. As we mentioned earlier, nothing else will matter as much as the drug itself. At this juncture, an actual relationship exists, but it's the kind of relationship which singularly seeks to dominate, manipulate, control, and entrap.

It is certainly not a healthy relationship. Remember Richard Pryor's comedy album entitled: "Richard Pryor: Live On The Sunset Strip. He recounts his nearly fatal brush with cocaine as a result of accidentally setting himself on fire when he was freebasing.

He vividly describes how he felt like his pipe was, "talking" to him. Richard told his story in his own hilarious way, but his story also contained an awesome element of truth; cocaine gradually became his lover, confidant, and trusted friend. Cocaine initially provides one with an incredible sense of "having it all together." The promise of a quick, readily available attainment of this sense seems irresistibly appealing to African American men with no definitive sense of who they are or what they are capable of becoming.

This is not to imply that these men become addicted to cocaine because of, for example, some unresolved childhood trauma. A self-destructive obsession to take cocaine can occur in the presence of gross family dysfunction or other circumstances. We would argue instead that these men have bought into the prevailing cultural myths which consistently emphasize the preeminence of individual success and achievement over anything else.

Furthermore, we would also argue that these men have adopted societal expectations as their very own. As Staples (1982) reports:

> "It is difficult to think of a more controversial role in American society than that of the Black male. He is a visible figure on the American scene, yet the least understood and studied of all sex-race groups in the United States. His cultural image is usually one of several types: the sexual superstud, the athlete, the rapacious criminal. That is how he is perceived in the public consciousness, interpreted in the dominant media and ultimately how he comes to see and internalize his own role. Rarely are we exposed to his more prosaic role as worker, husband, father, and American citizen. Even when he might be applauded for acts of heroism, as in the disproportionate number of Black men who served in the Vietnam war, public approbation eludes him because the war effort was both criminal and unsuccessful."

The emotional vacuum created by the appar-

ently compelling need to conform to these stereo-
types leaves one with no concrete sense of self.
Instead, what emerges is a pathetic caricature more
in line with Akbar's (1991) five D's for what can
characterize psychologically crippled or "dead"
African American men: deviant, devastated, de-
stroyed, destitute, and desecrated. Akbar goes on
to declare that African American men would do
well to study the lives of some of our greatest
African American men in order to know what it
truly means to be a man. They were as follows:
1) The Courage of Dr. King,
2) The Defiance of the Honorable Elijah Muhammad,
3) The Economic Strategy of Booker T. Washington,
   and perhaps the least known of these men,
4) The Uncompromising Integrity of Paul Robeson.

   There is no question that the lives of these men
can illuminate us with pivotal truths. Their collective character stands as excellent testaments to the
latent potential inherent in all African American
men.

   King, Muhammad, Washington, and Robeson
reached the pinnacle of who they were as African
American men. Their leadership, vision, and desire
effectively served to minimize the power of the emotional vacuum that all African American men are
especially prone to experience. When we consider
the wrenching plight of cocaine dependent African
American men and their quest to break free from
the debilitating chains of their addiction, we must
courageously ask what we would define as a rather
compelling question: how can we maintain an ad-

equate sense of self without the progressively dete-
riorating reliance upon cocaine to provide one with
that sense of self?

It is this urgent question that infuses our sense
of mission and purpose and forms the basis for our
discussion in subsequent chapters. We believe that
current research perspectives on African American men coalesce around the following eight paradigms:
1) Pathology-Deviance perspectives,
2) Acculturation-Victimization perspectives,
3) Oppression perspectives,
4) Coping philosophies,
5) Help-Seeking philosophies,
7) Criminality-Victimization viewpoints and,
8) Social Support concepts.

Each of these eight areas will be discussed in
view of how its own theoretical framework would
approach the phenomenon of cocaine dependent
African American men. I will argue that the Coping,
Africentrist, and Help-Seeking perspectives hold
tremendous promise for effective treatment and
recovery for cocaine dependent African American
men.

THE ECONOMICS OF ADDICTION

The African American communities' economic
resources are steadily evaporating under the awesome weight of cocaine dependence. In 1988, The
National Institute on Drug Abuse conducted a
household survey of illegal drug use by race and
sex. Sadly, as the following table indicates, African

66

American men topped the category for "ever used. " This chart uses information derived from The National Institute on Drug Abuse's 1988 breakdown of drug users by race, sex, and national origin. The survey asked about use of marijuana, cocaine, inhalants, hallucinogens, and heroin.

WHO'S USING DRUGS?	Ever Used	Used in Past Month	Used in Past Year
Black Men	43.6%	16.8%	10.2%
White Men	39.4%	15.8%	8.6%
Hispanic Men	37.8%	17.7%	9.9%
White Women	34.8%	12.1%	5.5%
Black Women	29.6%	10.5%	5.8%
Hispanic Women	28.9%	11.7%	6.5%

Source: Atlanta Journal/Constitution, Tuesday, August 7, 1990

The economic viability of African American men, and, by implication, what he could contribute to the edification of his community as well as his weakened ability to contribute to our community's sense of economic wellness and viability can be extrapolated from these figures. As Nobles and Goddard (1989) assert:

"Drugs and the drug culture are making it extremely difficult for the African American population to attain parity on economic and social levels. African Americans spend on the average $11-$12 billion annually on alcohol. The cost of illicit drugs is equally staggering. It is estimated that the average crack user spends $100 per week on crack. Assuming one percent of the African American population is using crack, at the average cost of $100 per week, the African American community is losing $655 million (126,000 x $5,200) a year to crack alone."

Life's opportunities and other "bankable" resources within our African American communities are gravely jeopardized by the devastation created by drug abuse and addiction. Again, Nobles and Goddard's (1989) analysis drive home some penetrating truths:

"The economic drain of substance abuse on the African American community could be better seen if we were to project it in terms of alternate resource allocation. For example, the low estimate of substance abuse treatment cost ($16 billion) could provide full four-year scholarships to Spelman or Morehouse College for 451,773 African American children per year. In fact, the low estimated substance abuse treatment cost could provide each of the 101 Historically Black Colleges with an annual endowment of $5 million for the next 30 years. For the estimated nine million African American persons living in poverty, this low estimated treatment cost could provide full health coverage annually in a Health Maintenance Organization. Applying the process to housing, the low estimated treatment cost could purchase 200,000 four bedroom homes (at $80,000 per home) annually for use by the homeless."

CRACK COCAINE AND VIOLENCE

The epidemic of violence so closely associated with the entry of crack cocaine into a consuming community is absolutely staggering. Victims and their murderers are overwhelmingly young African American males. Let's examine the relationship between the pharmacology of cocaine, the violence related to the craving to consume cocaine in the addicted individual, and the violence associated with the paranoid delusional syndromes so common with continued cocaine use.

Cocaine possesses a remarkable ability to induce symptoms like irritability, aggression, and paranoia in persons who are not necessarily predisposed to exhibit these symptoms. Because of the relationship between the melanin present in all African American men, the effects of cocaine may persist for days after one's last use.

Unpredictable hyperviligence, belligerence, and suspiciousness rapidly becomes pronounced and all-consuming as one seeks to satisfy the compulsive quest to take cocaine. Gradually, a cocaine-induced paranoid delusional syndrome becomes evident; one loses the ability to sort out reality from that which is patently false. Three cases from the March, 1987 issue of the *Drug Abuse Newsletter* are illustrative of some of the all too common scenarios:

I. THE CASE OF RECIPROCAL PARANOIA

Mike and Joe had been snorting cocaine for a couple of years. They were small-scale dealers, second order relatives and good friends. As time went on, Mike noticed occasions when he "got sick in the head" and experienced strong beliefs that people were going to kill him and his family. He also had compelling thoughts that he should kill Joe and the others who were plotting to do him in. These ruminations only occurred when he was on cocaine. He brought a rifle to protect himself, and when he was "sick" he usually stayed home afraid to go out, with a weapon always close by. One day, Joe angrily accused Mike of turning his wife on to cocaine and of having sex with her. So far as can be determined, this was an innocent accusation. Nevertheless, it made Mike even more suspicious during his paranoid intervals that Joe intended to harm him. Mike came to the conclusion that it was Joe who was playing around with his wife (probably a delusional notion). One day after having sniffed some cocaine, Mike got his rifle and drove his car to Joe's house. Joe happened to be in the front yard. He walked over to the car, Joe was heard to say: "Go home, take a rest. You're upset." Mike fired. [Joe was shot and killed]. Mike then proceeded to a pool hall where Joe's brother and another man, whom he did not like and whom he owed money, were known to hang out. He fired a number of shots into the pool hall, killing an adolescent and severely wounding a man, neither of whom were the intended victims. Mike said later that he wanted to kill Joe's brother, because he knew he would surely avenge his brother's death. Since being jailed, Mike has had no further episodes of paranoid thought disorder.

II. PATHOLOGICAL JEALOUSY

Jim was a compulsive freebase smoker. He no longer seemed to get much pleasure from using, but nevertheless persisted despite obvious severe weight loss, visual hallucinations that were very disturbing and an inability to work satisfactorily. He was fired from his job, but did not mind because it gave him the opportunity to stay home and watch his wife. According to Jim, she was exceedingly skillful at contacting a series of lovers in the hall and laundry room of their apartment building. Her protestations only served to reinforce the conviction that she was consistently unfaithful. He was never able to catch any of her lovers in the act, but he had seen strange men in the building. Furthermore, he blamed his impotence on her promiscuity. After Jim made a serious threat with a kitchen knife, his wife, Joan, became very upset and called a psychiatrist to ask for help. She wanted Jim "put away." It was explained that under state law, he might be detained for three days since he was mentally intact except for his single delusion. She would have to sign a complaint, and Jim would be even more suspicious and angry with her when he was released. It was suggested that she contact the police. She had already done this but the police were unwilling to make an arrest without actual evidence of harm. Jim was also unwilling to obtain treatment; he claimed that it was Joan who needed treatment. It was suggested to Joan that she leave the city and go to a place where Jim could not find her.

III. ACUTE PARANOIA CAN BE HARMFUL TO YOUR HEALTH

The victim, Henry, was a nasal cocaine user and a dealer. Often when he used cocaine even in moderate amounts, he had illusions (heard a car backfire and believed that people were shooting at him), hallucinations (heard voices and

71

sounds coming from the addict), and delusions (people were trying to steal his cocaine). He was not suspicious about his common-law wife or his three-year-old child, and when he was off cocaine for a few days, the paranoid notions subsided. One evening, he went out to the local bar, had a drink and met two strangers who seemed to be compatible. He invited them home for some beer and they had a good but noisy time. His wife complained that they were waking the sick baby, and when they did not quiet down, she left for her parents' home with the child. Henry continued to snort coke and drink some beer. By this time, the guests were quite drunk. Suddenly, Henry grabbed his shotgun, which was kept under the bed and ordered the two strangers out, while asking what they were doing there. Instead of leaving, one of the guests seized the shotgun and blew a hole in Henry's chest.

It is sobering to note that U.S. murders peaked at 23,044 in 1980, and actually declined to a total of 18,692 in 1984. The U.S. murder rate has quickly escalated with the introduction of crack cocaine on the American scene. The accelerating level of violence has produced an alarming weapons race; hence, the murder rate has skyrocketed. Common scenarios include:

In a typical sequence in the East New York wasteland of Brooklyn, two young hoods ("mutts" in police parlance) tried to rob a dealer named Johnny in an abandoned building. He killed them both. Two days later Johnny was found on the same scene, murdered in revenge by a friend of the dead pair. Given cases like that, cynics tend to shrug: bad people are killing each other, so why try to stop them? In Memphis, Tennessee, a suspected dealer named "Gangster Greg" Williams was booked in the fatal shooting of a buyer, posted $20,000 bond and then allegedly killed another man who was himself awaiting trial for murder. Gangster Greg is free again on $50,000 bond, but Memphis police are philosophical. "Sooner or later," says homicide Lt. Don Hollie, "somebody will shoot Greg, too."

MELANIN AND ADDICTION

Any relevant examination of the bondage which entraps cocaine dependent African American men would have to include some mention of a highly intriguing, though as yet, underdeveloped appreciation for the fascinating linkages between melanin and the addictive properties of cocaine.

Melanin is the chemical that produces skin color, the dark hues that makes us so brilliantly beautiful as African Americans. Carol Barnes (1988) has noted that two chemicals (in this instance, cocaine and melanin) with similar structures will automatically react to one another once electromagnetic contact is made in the brain. It is further assumed that the chemical binding of melanin (which we are so wonderfully blessed to have an abundance of) with the chemical properties of cocaine ultimately combine to produce effects within the basic brain chemistry of the addicted individual which are genuinely astonishing.

Carol asserted that this binding process is literally irreversible because the cocaine will inevitably "co-polymerize" into our melanin's chemical structures. Hence, the cocaine which we have taken will stay within the melanin centers within our bodies for what may become an indefinite period of time. It can be reasonably argued that the cocaine dependent African American male's quest for recovery from the steadily debilitating effects of addiction will be fraught with more pain, more difficulty, and more heartaches - precisely because of the very substance responsible for our Blackness - melanin.

Barnes explains, "When the body has completely used up the cocaine and it realizes that the natural chemicals (Melanin, serotonin, dopamine, etc.) are not available for regular body metabolism, it triggers a reaction called "craving". This craving forces the individual to acquire more of the intoxicating drug. (This is where crime comes into the picture.) The body has really been tricked into thinking that the cocaine chemical is melanin, serotonin, etc., due to the similarities in chemical structure".

This is why it's so extraordinarily compelling to gaze upon an African American male, formerly addicted to cocaine, who has allowed God to restore him to his rightful place. The physical countenance of that same male will necessarily radiate with power, integrity, beauty, and grace. Interestingly enough, King (1990) says that melanin also affects our memory and that it represents a pathway to the incredible riches of the "collective unconscious" among persons of African descent. He says:

"Thus, when we consider the biological features of melanin, its memory storage and capacity, its presence in old brain centers, increased brain pigmentation in more advanced biological species, and innumerable reports of persons with detailed memory images of ancient historical concepts; the evidence is indeed overwhelming."

Wilson (1981) also addressed himself to the significance of melanin:

"We have learned now in psychology that melanocyte [melanin] stimulating hormones can add significantly to the memory power of the individual."

Indeed, we can argue quite persuasively that cocaine dependence is clearly antithetical to the healing principles of Africentricity because it prevents our access to the revitalizing potential of the "ancient historical concepts." These ancient historical concepts include an abiding appreciation for the collective cultivation and development of the African mind. Cocaine singularly ruins one's attempt to sharpen the mind for intellectual or spiritual pursuits, enslaves, and ultimately destroys one's attempt to remain true to the unerasable mandate for excellence so inherent in the ancient historical concepts.

King was right on target: "The Black person who embraces their historical Blackness has the key to transforming the Black mind." On a negative note, Wilson (1981) also reported that melanin may also contribute "to the speed at which the nervous system operates." Cocaine is well known as a central nervous system stimulant and that taking cocaine can suddenly hurl our systems into very rapid overload.

This results in cardiac arrests and convulsions which can prove fatal. Therefore, the risk of sudden death from cocaine dependence is actually heightened considerably for African Amernican men by virtue of the way in which melanin accelerates its already profound effect on our central nervous systems.

PATHOLOGY/DEVIANCE PERSPECTIVES

This perspective emphasizes that African American men are inherently inferior to everyone else. Perceived deficits, faults, and limitations are emphasized as utterly unique to African American men. Interestingly enough, these views have a long history. They were especially pervasive in the 19th century. Rapid social changes, such as the gut-wrenching efforts to legislatively abolish the horrible institution of slavery, as well as efforts to achieve racial integration, were thought to increase "psycho-pathology" in African American men.

Freedom was curiously equated with the potential formal adjustment. Restrictive guidelines for regulating the behavior of African American men was equated with "community stabilization." During the latter years of the 19th century, researchers holding to a view of African American men as inferior published a number of studies which sought to highlight and promote racial differences.

One well-known example of an attempt to maintain the institution of slavery occurred during the 6th United States Census of 1840, the first federal census which sought to count the number of "psychologically deranged" persons. Using grossly misleading figures, this Census tried to show that the incidence of psychological maladjustment and depravity among African American slave populations in the South was only 1 in 1,558 compared to 1 in 162.4 in the free states of the North.

Therefore, the proponents of slavery theorized that African American men needed to be kept in bondage in order to prevent the emergence of psychological disorders among themselves. Slavery was therefore viewed as a civilizing agent. In contrast, psychological disorders among African Americans in the Northern free states were more pronounced because of the absence of slavery.

African American men in the North were thought to be incurably deranged. Only the institution of slavery could prevent him from exercising his abilities for autonomy, assertiveness, and collective empowerment. It was argued (Thomas & Sillen, 1972) that African American men functioned best when they were forcibly kept within the limits of their handicaps and that they became psychologically maladjusted whenever they were thrust into any kind of competitive arena.

It can be argued that remnants of these beliefs are evident today. For example, African American men in the work place may discover that their performance is incessantly monitored, checked, and supervised due to the assumption that they would commit serious blunders without the imposition of tight controls. The early evolution of clinical psychology also supported pathology/deviance perspectives on African American men.

Carl Jung, one of the world's most revered figures in the history of psychology, felt that African Americans were irredeemably below White men in every facet of existence.

Pathology/Deviance perspectives were also echoed by some influential social scientists that the accomplishments of the Civil Rights movement led to a rapid acceleration in the rate of psychiatric disorders among African American men. Moreover, bigoted thinking classified these disturbances exclusively by race. For example, let's look at how the phenomenon of depression and suicide were viewed. It was commonly believed that African American men were immune to the ravages of depression because of their inherently jovial and uncomplicated dispositions.

Bevis (1921) blithely declared: "Naturally, most of the race are carefree, live in the here and now with a limited capacity to recall or profit by experiences of the past. Sadness and depression have little part in his psychological makeup."

In this same vein, it is interesting to note that one of the most enduring images of African American men revolves around the character of Sambo.

Boskin (1986) asserts: "The entertaining grin was just one aspect of a large notion, the presumption that Sambo was an overgrown child at heart. And as children are given to presumptuous play, humorous antics, docile energies, and uninhibited expressiveness, so too one could locate in Sambo identical traits. Thus, the American national jester was a childlike figure whose enticing abilities centered on working and entertaining, producing and laughing, servicing and grinning." Boskin is also on target when he writes:

"Sambo was an extraordinary type of social control, at once extremely subtle, devious, and encompassing. To exercise a high degree of control meant also to be able to manipulate the full range of humor; to create, ultimately, an insidious type of buffoon. To make the Black man into an object of laughter was to strip him of masculinity, dignity, and self-possession. Sambo was, then, an illustration of humor as a device of oppression, and one of the most potent in American popular culture. The ultimate objective for Whites was to effect mastery: to render the Black male powerless as a potential warrior, as a sexual competitor, as an economic adversary."

It was also believed that suicide occurred primarily among depressed people. Since it was falsely assumed that African American men "were not inclined" toward depression, but were principally oriented toward childishness, silliness, and docility, suicide was thought to be non-existent. Prange and Vitols (1962) noted that Southern physicians considered suicide attempts by African Americans as irrefutable proof of White ancestry.

It is also important to note that this period in American social science history also witnessed the emergence of censorious attitudes on the use of an increasingly scary substance in American culture--cocaine. A 1908 article in the *New York Times* entitled "The Growing Menace of Cocaine" flatly declared that cocaine, "wrecks its victims more surely than opium" and that it was popular among Negroes in the South.

In September 1901 the topic of "Negro Cocainists" was openly addressed at the American Pharmacological Association. The Association's Committee on the Acquirement of the Drug Habit reported in 1903 that, "The Negroes, the lower and criminal classes are naturally most readily influenced by cocaine," and that, "Indiana reports that a good many Negroes and a few White women are addicted to cocaine." It soon became apparent that racial issues, though sometimes subsumed under the guise of the fear of crime, figured quite prominently in the accelerating quest to condemn cocaine.

Interestingly enough, opium has been associated with the Chinese in early attempts to prohibit it; cocaine was now inextricably linked with the "debauchery" of the African American male. Whites assumed that cocaine gave African American men a manipulative spirit and extraordinary strength.

Some Whites even believed that cocaine made "Negro men" immune to bullets (Erickson, et. al., 1985) which only contributed to their innate tendencies to commit utterly atrocious acts of violence. Perceived acts of violence against one of the most revered symbols in Southern culture - the White woman - were especially condemned.

Therefore, the "cocaine-crazed Black male dope fiend's" role in the burgeoning campaign to prohibit the presence of cocaine in American society was pivotal. Unfortunately, pathology/deviance models are still very much in use, e.g., Willie Horton and the 1988 Bush Presidential Campaign.

Pathology/Deviance perspectives are of no use as a model for aiding African American men ravaged by cocaine dependency. This blaming the victim mindset clearly represents a belief in the inability of African American men to act in an empowering fashion.

ACCULTURATION/VICTIMIZATION PERSPECTIVES

Persons subscribing to this view on African American men have argued that we have irretrievably relinquished any remnants of African American culture because of the effects of slavery. Aldous (1969) and Rainwater (1970) have reported that no family, or for that matter, cultural stability, existed in African life. In essence, they believe that the legacy of the African American male as inherently savage and barbaric is closely associated with the so-called uncivilized culture of Africa. They also imply that these legacies are very much in evidence today.

For example, the accelerating rate of Black-on-Black homicide in nearly every major city in the United States is assumed to be related to the allegedly barbaric character of African life. Acculturation/victimization perspectives also theorize that African American men are simply victims of employment discrimination and educational inequality. In the absence of these influences, they argue that African American men are fundamentally comparable to White men.

This perspective would have absolutely no use for culturally specific intervention strategies because it would be assumed that African American men have no recognizably distinct culture.

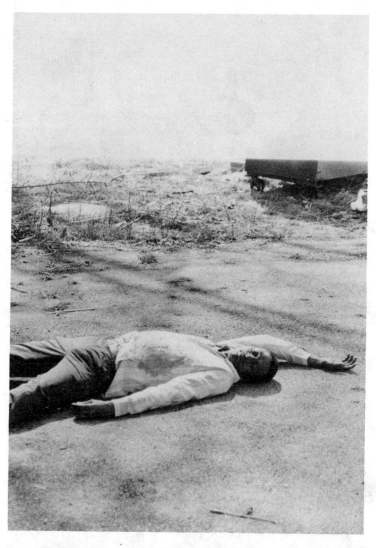

The U.S. murder rate has quickly escalated with the introduction of crack cocaine onto the American scene.

Drug usage is largely responsible for the displacement of Black men as heads of their household.

CHAPTER THREE
LOOSENING THE
CHAINS

COPING PHILOSOPHIES

Research paradigms which stress the abilities of African American men to transcend oppressive obstacles are beginning to be featured more prominently in literature. Cocaine dependent African American men with sustained periods of sobriety would intrigue researchers with a strength/coping focus. Instead of looking at perceived deficits of African American men, might a more productive focus rest on a study of the avenues by which we maintain a sense of wholeness and balance in a society which sees us as less than human?

In 1986, Howard University's Institute for Urban Affairs and Research conducted a research study in conjunction with the Commission for Racial Justice of the United Church of Christ which sought to determine chief characteristics and primary coping methods of strong, competent, and viable African American families. The goals for this important study were outlined as follows:

1) To determine the critical factors and conditions that contribute to strong Black family life.
2) To identify strategies employed by families in resolving the problems of living.
3) To add to the knowledge base on strong families that would enhance and practice intervention with families that are in need of help.
4) To identify models of self-help strategies used by strong families.

Results from this study identified the following features as particularly evident in strong African American families:

* strong kinship bonds.
* an achievement orientation.
* good parenting skills as evidenced by sound parent/child relationships.
* a religious/philosophical orientation.
* an intellectual/cultural orientation.
* an ability to deal effectively with stressful situations.
* clearly defined roles.
* high self-esteem.
* pride in their own accomplishments, as well as the accomplishments of other Black people.
* great enthusiasm for life.
* an emphasis on problem solving through discussions.
* high number of skills and talents within their households.

An emphasis on strengths would guide the delivery of effective rehabilitative services to African American men. Persons working in treatment centers would be oriented toward a process of enhancing attributes and qualities of African Americans which may lie dormant due to cocaine dependence.

OPPRESSION PERSPECTIVES

This perspective categorically rejects so-called psychological deficits of African American men. Here, negative structural arrangements in society are cited for why African American men have problems. Neo-conservatism, internal colonialism, and institutional racism are seen as prime causes to the worsening portrait of African American men.

Significantly enough, when we consider the concept of addictive disease as applied specifically to the phenomena of cocaine dependent African American men, oppression perspectives can become very seductive when we seek to explain the origins of dependency from this framework. For instance, Bell (1990) argues that the chemical dependency treatment field typically adheres to one of two primary theories about addiction; the disease theory and the environmental-secondary theory.

Proponents of the disease theory of addiction would speculate that cocaine dependency is a bona-fide disease that has a physical and a psychological component. The physical part of the disease theory is assumed to include one's genetic predisposition to addictive disease as well as how repeated drug use creates chemical alterations in brain functions - which in turn serves to disrupt one's thought processes and their abilities to cope effectively with life's problems.

The psychological component exists because the African American men may have tried to use cocaine, as we had mentioned earlier, to feel empowered. However, they gradually learn with a profound sense of shame, that cocaine remains fundamentally powerless to generate a true sense of empowerment in anyone.

Indeed, a sense of disempowerment becomes more and more grave. Despite a dawning awareness that cocaine does not possess the capacity to enable one to assume, for example, a proactive stance toward life, use of cocaine continues in the belief that it ultimately can.

Washton (1989) says that there are several advantages to viewing cocaine dependency as a disease. Implications for the recovery of cocaine dependent African American men also become clear:

(1) It helps to crystallize the rationale for abstaining from all mood-altering drugs. When an addict accepts the existence of his/her vulnerability to drugs and understands that it can be triggered by any drug use whatsoever, he/she will probably be better able to forego any opportunities for use (exposure). The argument of "My problem is with cocaine - not alcohol or marijuana - so I should be able to keep drinking or smoking pot as long as I stay away from cocaine" loses validity when he/she understands

that a relapse to cocaine addiction can be triggered by the use of any mood-altering substance whatsoever and that recovery from the addictive disease is impossible as long as drug use of any type continues. It no longer seems as though the treatment program or counselor is simply trying to take away anything that's fun by applying rigid rules about abstinence arbitrarily and dogmatically. The addict can begin to embrace the need to avoid the broad category of all mood-altering drugs, in much the same way some people must avoid dairy products because their digestive system cannot handle them. (2) Once the addicted individual accepts that the vulnerability is within him/herself, whether due to inherited predisposition or to repeated drug taking itself, he/she can begin to accept personal responsibility for making the behavioral and lifestyle changes necessary to achieve and maintain abstinence, by avoiding high-risk situations, by attending to negative mood states that can be precursors to relapse, in short, by doing everything possible to avoid re-exposure to their allergic agent, cocaine, and any other mood-altering drugs. (3) An understanding that drug addiction is a disease and that loss of control is a symptom of the disease can lift a great burden of guilt from the addict and thereby freeing up more constructive energy to be channeled into recovery rather than self-pity. No longer must he/she harbor unbearable feelings of weakness and worthlessness for having succumbed to addiction. This in turn makes it far easier to admit to and accept the addiction, for now being an addict is not such a self-indictment. One reason for the fierce denial in addiction may be that facing and admitting the problem mean getting in touch with deep-seated feelings of shame related to the stigma of being an addict. Cognitively reframing the addiction problem as a disease that is out of one's control and for which one is not to blame helps to lessen this stigma. The patient can then more easily say, "I am an addict," without feeling it is synonymous with saying, "I am a bad and worthless person." Commonly heard among recovering people in the rooms of Cocaine Anonymous (CA), Alcoholics Anonymous (AA) and other self-help programs is the saying, "I'm not a bad person getting good but a sick person getting better." For the vast majority of addicts, then, coming to view oneself as a sick person does not become an excuse for staying sick. It becomes a starting place from which to get better. (4) Recognizing that the disease is both physical and psychological helps the recovering addict see the importance not only of staying off drugs but also of making permanent changes in lifestyle, attitude, and behavior. Recovery from addictive disease is defined as the process of developing an entirely new, healthier way of living and being."

Advantage number three would seem to be particularly relevant for cocaine dependent African American men. Everyone who has ever had any kind of relationship with these men would readily testify to the strong presence of denial of the addiction - even in the face of overwhelming evidence to the contrary. However, how many of us can relate to how difficult it must be for these men to finally acknowledge the existence of a shame-based core within themselves that may function as an integral piece of their addictive process?

Isn't it already hard for us as African American men to come to terms with the very notion of being stigmatized in the first place, without having to wrestle with the unimaginable burden of a debilitating dependence upon cocaine?

Adherents to the environmental-secondary theory of addiction would be much more likely to espouse a belief in the power of external forces to cause African American men to slide into a dependence upon cocaine, or for that matter, any other addictive substance. A perfect example is the prevalence of alcohol abuse and alcohol dependency in the African American community.

Those persons who believe that environmental-secondary factors cause these problems in African American men could point to some rather compelling evidence to support their claims. For example, in a pivotal work entitled *Marketing Booze to Blacks* (1987) Hacker, Collins, and Jacobson assert:

"Despite high levels of alcohol problems, Blacks have become a special market for alcohol producers. Advertising targeted at Blacks, frequently utilizing the insights of Black-run advertising agencies, employs all media with particular emphasis on radio, Black-oriented magazines and inner-city billboards. One consequence of these heavy advertising expenditures has been the unwillingness of revenue-dependent Black publications to report on risks associated with alcohol use and abuse. Advertising campaigns are reinforced by a wide range of promotional activities, including sponsorship of concert tours, community sporting events, beauty contests, etc. Black celebrities are frequently featured. These alcohol promotions overwhelm the occasional messages publicizing health problems related to alcohol. Part of the alcohol marketer's strategy includes "reputation development" in the Black community. Alcohol companies sponsor such events as "Black History Month" or award dinners for well-known leaders. Their contributions to Black civic and community organizations and scholarships funds are generous compared to most other companies, and their assistance to Black economic development is a model for other industries. This largesse has placed many Black civic and political leaders in a bind. In return for accepting the contributions, they are forced to abstain from taking effective action to reduce alcohol problems in the Black community and to acquiesce in alcoholic beverage company marketing efforts designed to increase Black drinking."

Indeed, we are undeniably, even unabashedly targeted by these alcohol marketers. But an uncomfortable question raises its threatening head: must we succumb to the these messages, though admittedly insistent, that we give in to these temptations? Bell (1990) even goes so far as to say: "While it is clear that there are strong institutional, economic, and cultural roadblocks that impede recovery, it is hard to imagine an individual or cultural group, [in this case, African American men] making significant progress in addressing alcohol and other drug use while viewing it as only a secondary problem."

I believe that Mr. Bell is right on target. Recall Washton's observations relative to the advantages of viewing addiction as a valid disease. Bell also argues that if oppression perspectives were responsible for producing chemical addictions among African American people, then the rates of addiction among us would have been much greater in the past because racism was legally sanctioned and more obvious than it is today.

Indeed, the rates of addiction among African American families prior to the shift from an agrarian to an industrialized society was largely insignificant because of the primacy of the family. Helping traditions in African American families, long cherished as an ingredient considered essential to the very survival of our families, gradually began to be replaced by a self-centered system of values which, interestingly enough, makes one more prone to the development of all kinds of maladies.

Martin and Martin (1985) validate this point in their discussion of how helping traditions were diluted:

> "The individualistic adaptation of Blacks to the city has become the dominant attitude of a number of hard-working, striving Blacks who have managed to achieve middle-class status through legitimate means. Adopting a competitive, individualistic, social Darwinistic stance, the efforts of these Blacks focused largely on improving their well-being and that of their immediate family and excluded most activities that involved helping other Blacks. In earlier generations, this stance was expressed by pa-

triarchy. In strong patriarchal Black families, the man was likely to view himself as an exceptional Negro - as the one out of a million who made it not by the help of others, he would claim, but by his own initiative and drive. Most significantly, he was likely to view himself as a man whose wife did not have to work, which was the general standard by which Black men judged their success as patriarchs. He was apt to have no pity for those Black men who had not "made it" or whose wives had to work outside the home. He was apt to be conservative and hostile toward helping other Blacks or being helped by them, preferring to identify with and do the bidding of the White ruling class rather than join oppressed Black men and women in a common struggle."

Interestingly enough, oppression perspectives have been used to describe how alcohol was employed to minimize the chances for slave revolts. Preeminent African American abolitionist Frederick Douglass (1892) declared that slave holders would consistently attempt to get slaves to consume alcohol because of the belief that "drunk slaves" could not plan insurrections.

Williams (1986) noted that unemployment, always higher for African American men, is connected with the development of alcohol problems.

Can we argue that a return to a system of values more in keeping with our African traditions would enrich the lives of cocaine dependent African American men? It is this question that constitutes the focus of our next section.

AN AFRICENTRIC FRAME OF REFERENCE

Researchers with an Africentrist view have focused their attention on the dynamics through which African American men use adaptive modes of cultural expression to oppression. So-called maladaptive reactions to oppression are simply not promoted. Thus, according to Asante, (1991) Africentricity is a genuinely liberating ideology with enormous implications. He declares:

> "Africentricity is the centerpiece of human regeneration. To the degree that it is incorporated into the lives of the millions of Africans on the continent and in the Diaspora, it will become revolutionary. It is purposeful, giving a true sense of destiny based upon the facts of history and experience. The psychology of the African without Africentricity has become a matter of great concern. Instead of looking out from one's own center, the non-Africentric person operates in a manner that is negatively predictable. The person's images, symbols, lifestyles, and manners are contradictory and thereby destructive to personal and collective growth and development. Unable to call upon the power of ancestors, because one does not know them; without an ideology of heritage, because one does not respect one's own prophets; the person is like an ant trying to move a large piece of garbage only to find that it will not move."

Martin and Martin (1985) have asserted that the helping traditions (so very synonymous with the principles of Africentricity) once so evident in African American families, i.e., mutual aid, social class

and status cooperation, male/female equality, pro-social behavior, fictive kinship, racial consciousness and religious consciousness, have been replaced by the following four ideologies; all of which stand opposed to the healing properties of Africentricity: 1) an enormous emphasis on individualism, 2) a singular focus on acquiring material items, social status, and money, 3) motivation is centered on one's own escape from the hardships of poverty, and finally, 4) values are centered exclusively on European traditions. In contrast, Asante (1991) says that helping, healing, and healthy relationships within African American communities which are founded on the healing energies of Africentric principles are characterized by four elements:
1.) sacrifice
2.) inspiration
3.) vision
4.) victory

SACRIFICE
Africentricity requires that relationships become sacrificial in tone and quality. The advancement of other people assumes great importance; things are no longer characterized by an attitude of "as long as you and I are happy, that's all that matters." Asante says, "But like all sacrifices, Africentric sacrifice never really leaves us less. What seems to be a sacrifice always rebounds to happiness and joy. It gives us more than we had before."

INSPIRATION

Africentricity also requires that we become committed to, and stimulated by our interactions with our partners. We rejoice when they rejoice, and we weep when they weep. We take special pride in their achievements; we don't see ourselves as "less than."

VISION

An orientation toward the accomplishment of shared goals is an essential aspect of relationships based on Africentric principles. It is as Asante declares: "[Vision]... is the galvanizing element that keeps the relationship on track. To be able to ask, do you see and be assured that your partner does see the same vision provides a sense of communion. Commitment to a fundamental vision, a profound project, a spiritual quest, is the king of commitment which demonstrates vision."

VICTORY

Relationships based on the principles of Africentricity are victorious. Asante says that these relationships represent, "A celebration of ourselves, our aspirations, achievements, and accomplishments accompany the victorious aspect of a relationship. It is a relationship of joy, of power, of peace, of overcoming; it does not speak of failure, losses, of suffering and oppression. Victory means that you have won, not that you are expecting to win. Africentric relationships are victorious by nature. Being Africentric is being victorious."

Based on the above, can we assume that our abandonment of an Africentric frame of reference has led to an alarming increase in the rates of addiction among African American men?

Nobles, Goddard, Cavil and George (1987) have developed a model for understanding the fascinating linkages between African American families, the drug culture, and how those values contrast so dramatically with a West African frame of reference:

BLACK FAMILY ORIENTATION
I. **Cultural Themes**
   sense of appropriateness
   sense of excellence
   self-worth
II. **Cultural Value System**
   mutual aid
   adaptability
   natural goodness
   inclusivity
   unconditional love
   respect (for elders)
   restraint
   responsibility
   reciprocity
   interdependence
   cooperativeness

DRUG CULTURE VALUE ORIENTATION
I. **Drug Culture Themes**
   anything is permissible
   trust no one
II. **Drug Culture Value System**
   selfish
   materialistic
   pathological liar

extremely violent
short-fused
individualistic
manipulative
immediate gratification
paranoid
distrustful
non-family oriented
non-community oriented
quantity

Indigenous cultural adaptations, for example, core attitudinal beliefs, psychological coping styles, and expressive behavior patterns are believed to have not only been retained by African American men, but that these adaptations have been transmitted across generations.

Africentric perspectives would appear to hold great promise as an aid to the process of recovery for cocaine dependent African American men. Indeed, our solutions to the problems of cocaine dependency among these men will emerge primarily from this perspective.

SOCIAL SUPPORT CONCEPTS

Closely related to help-seeking perspectives, social support concepts within African American communities (the tangible and intangible forms of assistance that members of these communities receive from one another) are belatedly receiving increased attention from social science researchers and scholars (Billingsley, 1968; Stack, 1974; Belle, 1982).

Emotional and material supports provided largely by extended family members are traditionally viewed as a characteristic especially indigenous to us as African American people. However, recent research (McAdoo, 1982; Martin and Martin, 1985) would appear to suggest that these long-cherished traditions among us are gradually eroding.

This critically important development could have grave implications for attempts by the African American male to extricate himself from the grips of cocaine dependency. For example, two of the most historically important functions found in our families are what Martin and Martin (1985) called, "mutual aid". It is a process which according to the authors, "involves a reciprocal effort by family members to pool resources necessary for survival and growth," and "fictive kinship" which involves, "the care giving and mutual aid relationship among non-related Blacks that exists because of their common ancestry, history, and social plight."

The unarguably diminished power of these two value systems may partially explain why we as African Americans tend to access chemical dependency treatment programs at a time when our disease has reached a very advanced stage. Weakened systems of accountability, once entirely absent from our communities, may promote and/or enable African American men to remain entangled in the suffocating despair of their dependency. The following comments are not uncommon: "He's on drugs? Well, it's really not any of my business" or "As long as I'm not messed with or robbed, I really don't care."

Bell (1990) says that our noted tendency to access chemical dependency treatment programs at a later time has enormous implications. He writes:

"Later entry into treatment often means entering via the court system as opposed to self-referral or intervention by family or employer.

Later entry lowers the probability for successful treatment and long-term recovery. The alcoholic or other addict who comes to treatment late in the progression of the disease is less likely to have an intact, supportive family or a job, both of which are important predictors of recovery success.

Later entry is costly, since inpatient treatment is usually required.

Later entry increases the likelihood of diseases or physical malfunctions caused or exacerbated by chemical dependency."

As Bell asserts, a supportive family is vitally important to one's recovery. The active and sustained participation of family members in the treatment of cocaine dependent African American men is considered vital to the goal of achieving treatment success. Consequently, weakened family systems are detrimental to prospects of recovery for these men.

HELP-SEEKING PHILOSOPHIES

Help-seeking models are also receiving increased attention in the social science and mental health field (Hendricks, Howard and Gary, 1981; McKinlay, 1973; Milburn, 1987; Linn and McGranahan, 1980). The process of examining how potential recipients of social and mental health services access available resources becomes especially important when cocaine dependent African American men are considered.

Some of the most notable recent research on help-seeking behaviors among African American males was conducted by Gary, et. al. (1987). The data for their study was obtained from interviews of 142 African American males who were 18 years of age or older who resided in the Metropolitan Washington D.C. area. Gary, et. al., found that the majority of these men preferred to solve their own problems and that there was generally little use of normal sources of help, although these men seemed to be open to using them.

The results of this would appear to support prior research from a national study (Neighbors, 1981) which suggested that many African Americans use informal support systems during times of need, e.g., extended family members, friends, neighbors, and co-workers. The practical implications for substance abuse treatment centers would include the development of strategies to promote the inclusion of key extended family members in the recovery process.

CRIMINALITY/VICTIMIZATION VIEWPOINTS

Researchers who address themselves to the ways in which African Americans act out destructive cycles among ourselves seems to be a fairly new area of interest (Flowers, 1988). These researchers are actively searching for ways to explain the following facts:

- African American men face a 1 in 21 chance of being murdered during their life times compared to a 1 in 131 chance for White men (Flowers, 1988).

- Health officials now contend that the rate of murder among African American males (it remains as the leading cause of death between the ages of 15 and 24 for this population) is now so staggering that it should be considered a public health issue (Minsky, 1984).

Some of these researchers have said that self-destructive patterns among African Americans can be explained by certain socioeconomic advances. For instance, African American men may be acutely aware of opportunity structures, i.e., lower home interest rates, yet, because of racist practices, remain unable to truly take advantage of them. Feelings of disillusionment may set in, which may serve to heighten one's sense of vulnerability for substance abuse.

SUMMARY

In summary, each of the foregoing research perspectives have all sought to describe important issues pertaining to the life of African American men. Each perspective was discussed in terms of how its own theoretical base would approach the phenomenon of cocaine dependency among African American men. It can be seen that three of these perspectives: Coping, Africentric, and Help-Seeking hold great promise in terms of helping us to arrive at practical solutions to the problem.

Cocaine dependent African American men can network and draw strength from one another as they reveal their vulnerabilities.

CHAPTER FOUR
BLACK MEN
UNSHACKLED

COPING STRATEGIES

I had mentioned earlier that cocaine dependence gradually assumes that status of a true relationship, but with an ironic twist. Cocaine dependence contributes to the illusion of the perfect relationship by persuading its user to feel that a constant state of bliss is attainable and that the desired state for any good relationship lies in always feeling wonderful. Relationship problems may lead the user to feel that cocaine possesses an uncanny ability to make those problems go away.

However, the emotional tools required to maintain a good relationship become completely absent with the onset of cocaine dependence. I had mentioned as well that cocaine can make its user feel invulnerable and invincible. Now, it is exceedingly difficult at best for African American men to feel this way without cocaine anyway!

So, we go back to our question. How can African American men maintain a positive sense of who they are (marvelously created in the very image of

God) without cocaine? Some of the answers might be found in the Coping, Help-seeking, and Africentrist models described in earlier chapters. Let's begin by exploring what solutions may lie within the Coping perspective.

A rehabilitative approach which uses a coping model as its framework for treatment will look for ways to use whatever strengths cocaine dependent African American men possess for recovery, and indeed, if we look with new eyes, these strengths are quite numerous. Here, before treatment staff would be allowed to work with cocaine dependent African American men in recovery,they would be instructed in ways to effectively relinquish commonly held, largely pejorative views which interfere with sound treatment.

If we assume (and rightly so) that attitudes about African American men influence subsequent treatment decisions concerning the same, it then becomes so compelling that we courageously examine long held beliefs which may lie outside of our immediate awareness.

Therefore, one of the most important tasks that we can engage in as persons working with cocaine dependent African American men is to explore our own values and perceptions that, if left unexplored, will do nothing but impact negatively on our work with these men. Boyd-Franklin (1989) captures the essence of this continuous challenge by declaring that the process of joining, i.e., establishing a working alliance by building a relationship prior to the beginning of treatment represents the single

105

most important process in working clinically with African American families. She goes on to discuss how we as African Americans are acutely sensitive to what she defines as, "vibes":

"Black people, because of the often extremely subtle ways in which racism manifests itself socially, are particularly attuned to very fine distinctions among such variables in all interactions - with other Blacks with White people and with "White" institutions. Because of this, many Black people have been socialized to pay attention to all of the nuances of behavior and not just to the verbal message. The term most often applied to this multilevel perception in Black culture is "vibes". A clinician (whether Black or White) needs to be acutely aware that every Black client and family member is "checking out" her or him in terms of appearance, race, skin color, clothing, perceived social class, language, and a range of more subtle cues such as warmth, genuineness, sincerity, respect for the client, willingness to hear the client's side, patronizing attitudes, condescension, judgments, and human connectedness."

Other areas of exploration include one's examination of his or her own family and the role of men in that same family, the degree to which our families may have implemented empowerment strategies to alleviate the impact of racism and what "world view" was prevalent in the family. The multifaceted strengths of the African American church community could serve as a prime resource.

Also, self and collective empowerment strategies

(for example, cocaine dependent African American male patients would participate in the development of their own treatment plans) would seem to be in line with inherent strengths evident in all African American men. Let's turn our attention next to treatment insights from Help-Seeking Solutions.

HELP-SEEKING SOLUTIONS

Breaking the terrible cycle of dependency with cocaine dependent African American men with a "help-seeking" model would also appear to hold much promise. Again, African American men tend to use informal support systems during periods of need and these informal networks consist of co-workers, neighbors, friends, and extended family members.

We may legitimately assume that the majority of treatment programs fail to acknowledge this sense of supportive collectivism still evident in our culture. This failure is largely attributable to racist assumptions of what constitutes effective treatment, i.e., one treatment approach is good for all; African American men don't have an appreciably distinct culture.

However, persons working with cocaine dependent African American men in treatment settings must become educated on the specific imperatives of the need to cultivate a deep, rich, and abiding appreciation for how best to employ in the recovery process those persons who are integral members of the informal support network. One key need would rest with the importance of expanding one's definition of "family" whenever the culture of African American men is considered.

As I mentioned earlier, the concept of "fictive kinship" (Martin and Martin, 1985) is very real in the African American community. The relationship between the dynamics of fictive kinship and how this network of persons could function as a healing resource for African American men becomes especially crucial when we speak about recovery from the web of cocaine addiction.

Cocaine addiction is a problem that unquestionably affects all of the members of one's network or family. Mbiti says: "I am because we are, and since we are, therefore, I am." Therefore, frustration, rage, anger, or denial becomes increasingly prominent in the lives of those who comprise the network. These feeling are the result of watching the addict's relationship with cocaine progress to the point where all else is literally secondary.

Denial of the problem constitutes one of the most insidious manifestations that can actually serve to perpetuate the cycle of addiction. Washton declared that denial is most likely to happen among, "family members who may find that focusing on the addict provides them with a welcomed relief and distraction from their own problems, crises, and unhappiness." This process typically occurs outside of one's immediate awareness.

We believe that this dynamic becomes particularly compounded among and within members of the cocaine dependent African American male's network because of how difficult it is for us to acknowledge vulnerabilities of virtually any kind. Added to this difficulty is the profound sense of shame that arises within us if we were to admit to the reality of what the cocaine is doing to the addicted male.

Denial of the problem is closely associated with the process of enabling or how members of the network may unwittingly help to keep the addiction alive. Washton says that these behaviors can include the following:

> (1) Minimizing - rationalizing, ignoring, minimizing, or otherwise "explaining away" the addict's problem and its consequences: "It's not so bad, lots of people use drugs nowadays; "He's a troubled person. He's had a tough life and needs a chance to work out his problems before he can stop using drugs."
>
> (2) Controlling - attempting to manipulate or control the addict's drug supply and/or drug use, making bargains with the addict to be "good", bribing the addict to stop using drugs; giving the addict ultimatums, making idle threats, etc.
>
> (3) Shielding - protecting the addict from negative consequences of the addiction: making excuses, covering up, rescuing the addict from trouble, etc.
>
> (4) Taking over responsibilities - paying bills, performing household tasks, etc.
>
> (5) Colluding - helping the addict obtain drugs, giving the addict drugs.

When members of the network behave in this fashion, we have, in essence, neglected to remain true to the healing principles of corrective collectivism once so very evident in our culture as African Americans. Instead, we become engaged in a harmful process that can actually hasten the demise of the cocaine dependent African American male. The willingness to cease with enabling behaviors may serve to mar the beginning of real recovery because in the absence of previously available "supports" these men may finally confront the dreadful reality of their addiction for the first time.

Putting a halt to enabling behaviors does not mean that members of the addict's network should adopt a European-based, individualistic orientation toward the process of recovery. In fact, it is absolutely crucial that key members of the addict's network participate actively in the addict's program of recovery. To do so heightens the chances of achieving a successful treatment outcome.

Finally, let's turn our attention to what solutions may be gleaned from an Africentric point of view.

AFRICENTRIST IDEAS

We had mentioned before that an Africentrist view of cocaine dependency among African American men would assume that these men have abandoned, or are simply not in tune with a West African frame of reference in all three spheres: attitudinal, spiritual, and behavioral. In other words, drug use will emerge once we fail to appreciate and act upon values intrinsic to our nature as African American men.

Martin and Martin (1985) described some of the helping traditions found in ancient African cultures. In doing so, they captured some of the most fundamental principles of Africentricity:

"Blacks had a solid reputation for being polite, hospitable, and charitable long before they were brought to this country in slave ships. Park, one of the earliest European explorers of Africa, expecting to find Africans in a state of savagery and chaos, was startled by the high level of organization and civility among African people. He found that Africans from the most highly complex nation to the simplest tribal unit were not lacking in art, religion, trade, law, government, architecture, education, and other tangible and intangible products associated with a people fashioning their own culture and society. Park was particularly fascinated by and grateful for the warm hospitality extended to him by Africans during his travels."

Asante (1991) boldly declares that Africentricity, "... is a transforming power that helps to recapture the true sense of our souls." As African American men, one key aspect of our souls lies in our indomitable sense of harmony and oneness with mankind. This pivotal sense of relatedness with the whole of mankind, so startlingly evident in the African compassion for the European explorer many centuries ago, constitutes one of the most essential ingredients to the development of health and wellness models for African American men.

We had said before that an Africentric view of the problem of cocaine dependency among African American men would naturally assume that these men had abandoned, or at best, are simply not in tune with an Africentric frame of reference. Primary features of an Africentric perspective include (Asante, 1991):

Africentricity maintains intellectual vigilance as the proper posture toward all scholarship which ignores the origin of civilization in the highlands of East Africa.

Africentricity is the logical outgrowth of the collective conscious will of the people-the collective conscious wills derived from Africentricity.

Africentric vigilance is demanded to preserve our culture.

The Africentric drive to create must always be based on a deep, collective commitment to excellence.

Africentricity demands a commitment to greatness based upon the true historical character of the people.

Africentricity is a liberating ideology. A person who chooses to live an Africentric life will always transcend the mundane attitudes. To be Africentric is to be in touch with one's ultimate reality in every way.

The Africentric perspective envisions one wholistic, organic process. Thus, all political, artistic, economic, ethical, and aesthetic issues are connected to the context of Africentric knowledge. Everything that you do; all that you are and will become is intricately wrapped with the Kente of culture. Mind and matter, spirit and fact, truth and opinion are all aspects or dimensions of one vital process.

Interestingly enough, the erosion of Africentric principles coincides with our forced removal from Africa and enslavement in America. The power and timelessness of these remarkable principles, though certainly retained to some degree by virtue of the unshakable immutability of their truth, gradually waned in influence.

Bell (1990) observed that the emergence of chemical dependency tends to develop whenever rapid cultural dislocation occurs. Bell has also brilliantly asserted that how a community elects to answer the following six questions testifies to the presence of the potential for that same community to witness the emergence of chemical dependency problems:

1. What chemicals are legitimate to use?
2. Has the culture, community, or family established a context for chemical use.
3. Are there cultural institutions that can effectively establish and communicate alcohol and other drug use rules?
4. Are there clear cultural, community, or family systems of accountability?
5. Are there functional tools to cope with stress?
6. Are there functional rites of passage?

WHAT CHEMICALS ARE LEGITIMATE TO USE?

Bell correctly asserts that we have established no clear and consistent standards in our communities with regard to the use of alcohol and other drugs. Gutman (1976) has said that the African American family from 1750 to 1925 was a cultural, psychological, and spiritual unit in that it had an intact, cohesive, and clearly defined structure with two parents.

However, after 1925, pivotal developments altered the continued viability of our families. In the decades between 1940 and 1970, over four million African American families migrated from the South to the North. However, it was precisely during this same period that the African American family began to decline. We began to adopt the prevailing system of values found in Northern communities. In other words, our adherence to Africentric principles began to become diluted.

Nobles, Goddard, and Cavil (1985) have compared and contrasted differences between Africentric and European values in the following manner:

AFRICAN (Eastern)	EUROPEAN (Western)
Human manifestation of the supreme	Humans are created of (the product) the supreme
Human misconduct leads to separation from God	Contest of wills (man against the Divine)
Man determines (chooses) his own fate (destiny')	Man's destiny subject to the influence of a powerful other
Essential Functions:	**Essential Functions:**
Ideas of Will	**Ideals of Control**
Capacity to have will (thought) and creativity	Ability to manipulate
Ideas of Command	**Ideas of Domination**
Capacity to have intent and to produce that which it will	Ability to manage
Ideas of Ascension	**Ideas of Opposition**
Capacity to grow and develop	Ability to oppose or contrast
Ideas of Transformation	**Ideas of Separateness**
Capacity to change	Ability to define difference
Ideas of Transcendence	**Ideas of Powerlessness**
Capacity to renew and go beyond itself	Ability to fear

The absence of strong systems of account-ability, once so cherished, weakened the strengths of African American families, thereby making it more vulnerable to various contaminants. Prior to the great migration, alcohol and drug use was not a major threat to the stability of the African American community.

HAS THE CULTURE, COMMUNITY, OR FAMILY ESTABLISHED A CONTEXT FOR CHEMICAL USE?

Bell says that the African American community has not provided itself with direct, clear, and concise responses to the following questions:

a. When is it legitimate to use alcohol or other drugs?
b. Where is it legitimate to use alcohol or other drugs?
c. What behaviors should we tolerate from those who use alcohol and other drugs?

Question (c) would seem to be especially appro-priate for us as African American men because of the remnants of our once strong sense of "collective consciousness" among one another. In our commu-nities, drugs are still glamorized. This tendency toward glamorization would necessarily produce imprecise answers to question (c) Wade and God-dard (1989) have said:

"The mindset or group psychology surround-ing drugs and criminal activity in the urban community presents an especially complex cli-mate. In many ways drug dealers are revered, feared, respected, and despised all at the same

115

time. The picture this creates for African American children is understandably confusing.

For instance, the killing of a young African American man in Oakland who was involved in drug trafficking and drug-related criminal activity received national press coverage. Prior to his death, the local media profiled his life and ascension to "Kingpin" of the drug culture, giving him a "Robin Hood" aura or mystique. Reports of his illegal activities were almost always juxtaposed with the fact that he often fed hungry families, took groups of kids to amusement parks, tossed basketballs out to needy kids from his White Rolls Royce, etc. Upon his death, no other issue occupied the minds of the community. Partly due to the attention his death received from the press, an inordinate amount of discussion centered around the life and death of a convicted criminal and known drug dealer. Consequently, hundreds, if not thousands, of youth witnessed the power and importance of drug-related criminal activity when the casket of a criminal and deviant drug dealer was literally carried across the entire city by a horse-drawn glass hearse, followed by five White Rolls-Royce, a grey Rolls-Royce, a Silver Cloud, five grey Cadillacs, two White Lincoln Stretch Continentals, a Black Lincoln Limousine, and numerous other signs of prestige and importance."

The foregoing observations speak very poorly to our abilities to distinguish between appropriate and inappropriate behaviors among those who would "do drugs" in any capacity. Thus, we can only remain at risk.

ARE THERE CULTURAL INSTITUTIONS THAT CAN EFFECTIVELY ESTABLISH AND COMMUNICATE ALCOHOL AND OTHER DRUG USE RULES?

Bell says that there were three key institutions that had historically set the standards for chemical use and abuse rules; 1) religious leaders, 2) the family, and, 3) the state. We would like to comment on standard number one, religious leaders, or religious institutions. The African American church had historically functioned as the preeminent and uncontested voice in our communities.

However, the church has allowed itself in some respects to become influenced by value systems at odds with its mission of nurturing souls. The incorporation of individualistic tenets within the church may be seen as a prime example. This development has an ironic twist to it.

The use of spirituality in the treatment and recovery of cocaine dependent African American men is considered to be essential to successful treatment outcomes. Yet, can we not argue that the persuasive powers of the church have been critically diluted and contaminated? Will we turn to the church as a source of comfort and healing?

Spirituality which is individualistic in tone and practice is downright dangerous; spirituality must be practiced corporately.

ARE THERE CLEAR CULTURAL, COMMUNITY, OR FAMILY SYSTEMS OF ACCOUNTABILITY?

Internal mechanisms of accountability remain largely absent from our communities. Past family traditions, i.e., exercising the right and authority to discipline an African American child not biologically connected to you is now seen as an worn-out, dusty relic. Individualism has crept in to fill the void. The results can only be described as crippling and tragic.

ARE THERE FUNCTIONAL TOOLS TO COPE WITH STRESS?

The foundations of the African American community are now being rocked in an unprecedented fashion. Key developments are presented in a 1992 *Newsweek* article entitled "Losing Ground":

*African American children are three times more likely than White children to reside in a single-parent household. 43.2 percent of all African American children are living in the throes of poverty.

*African Americans presently account for 28.8 percent of all U.S. AIDS cases. African Americans comprise 52 percent of the women with the disease. African American children currently represent 53 percent of all pediatric AIDS cases. Have we developed practical solutions to the stresses engendered by this portrait? or have we via drugs and alcohol anesthetized ourselves into oblivion?

ARE THERE FUNCTIONAL RITES OF PASSAGE?

Rites of passage are commonly referred to as acts which support the movement from childhood, to adolescence, to adulthood. In ancient African societies, rites of passage were instrumental to the development and cultivation of brilliant minds. Some of the difficulties uniquely peculiar to African

American men should be viewed as behaviors which are out of sync with our historical and cultural roots.

We are in dire need of programs specifically designed to return us to an appreciation of our true characters as African people. Paul Hill, Jr. has written an excellent book, *Coming of Age: African American Male Rites of Passage* (1992), to stimulate the creation and implementation of rites of passage programs for our youth.

Rites of passage programs are closely associated with the need for internal systems of accountability and would go a long way toward the goal of reducing the incidence of drug abuse in our communities.

The healing traditions found within an Africentric frame of reference could provide us with the kinds of concrete answers to these six questions thereby providing us with a sound foundation for the development of practical solutions to the poignant dilemma of cocaine dependent African American men. In this regard, Asante (1991) unarguably declares that the legacy of Africentricity necessarily includes, "two aspects of consciousness: (1) toward oppression, and (2) toward victory."

As you review his thoughts on these two components, pay particular attention to his notion of "victorious consciousness" and its relationship to the liberation from cocaine dependence among African American men:

"When a person is able to verbalize the condition of oppression, he exhibits the earliest consciousness of his oppression. This is the most elemental form of consciousness and is found in the speeches, poems, plays and lives of a million people who parade as conscious individuals. They know neither the correct expression of consciousness nor the damage they do to their own persons by practicing a fractured consciousness."

He also says:
"... consequently, deliverance is postponed until there is a victorious historical will. The victorious attitude shows the Africans on the slave ship winning. It teaches that we are free because we choose to be free. Our choice is the determining factor, no one can be your master until you play the part of slave."

The concept of the "victorious historical will" so eloquently described by Asante, could be used as the quintessential principle that motivates the cocaine dependent African American male to liberate himself from the crushing nightmare of his addiction. The healing balm of the victorious will could become manifest in the following manner:

Since we operate from the premise that an addiction is intimately associated with our quest to find a deeper level of spirituality (May, 1989), stopping the cycle of cocaine addiction would mean that we must say "yes" to the outstretched arm of God. God's desire is that we enjoy the fruits of the victorious historical will; after all, this ultimately comes from Him in the first place.

The call to restfully abide in the midst of the victorious historical will is clearly synonymous with May's (1989) beautiful notion of the homeward call.

The homeward call is God's gentle invitation to us to return home to Him. When we make that decision to return home to Him, when we decide to claim the richness of our true heritage, (the victorious historical will), then God transforms our desire for cocaine into what it really represents anyway-an unshakable longing to find rest in His loving embrace.

May then says that at the moment that we decide to say "yes" to God, our struggle for deliverance from an addiction becomes consecrated or dedicated to God. It is also vitally important to note that our abilities to say "yes" to God are heightened considerably when we surround ourselves with, and become accountable to, a support network.

Our engagement in a support network is entirely in line with our traditions which place high value on "family". Moreover, positive developments occur once we submit ourselves to the primacy of this value. Once again, May is right on target:

"...God's grace through community involves something far greater than other people's support and perspective. The power of grace is nowhere as brilliant nor as mystical as in communities of faith. Its power includes not just love that comes from people and through people, but love that pours forth among people, as if through the very spaces between one person and the next. Just to be in such an atmosphere is to be bathed in healing power."

May has also asserted that groups (or, as in our case, informal support networks) can become consecrated. Can you imagine the awesome power of an African American support network that remains diligently committed to their inescapable, yes, inescapable mandate to participate in the process of liberation from cocaine? The chances for genuine liberation would be enhanced considerably because the support network would be acting in concert with the healing energies so inherent to true Africentricity anyway!

FAMILY SUPPORT AS A HEALING RESOURCE

In order to reinforce our quest for the design and implementation of genuinely liberating strategies from the bondage of cocaine addiction among African American men, we have argued that we must return to a system of values that rings out with the truth of africentric principles. Furthermore, we have stated that cocaine addiction can be viewed as an abandonment of our heritage as viable African American men.

Our reliance upon an Africentric framework for our liberation from the slavery of addictive disease fundamentally requires that we incorporate "family" into this life or death process. However, a delicate balance must be achieved between our tendencies to enable an addiction versus our loving detachment from it.

This balance is so very precious because our grounding in the principles of Africentricity would necessarily compel us to "become at one" with the addict. Let's share a common scenario of what cocaine can do to our families. We will then discuss the differences between the process of enabling (behaviors from family members which can actually serve to perpetuate an addiction) and the

Africentric mandate to live in close harmony with our families, even in the midst of the unspeakable pain of addiction.

Washton (1990) shares the following case illustration to show how cocaine addiction negatively impacts the whole family, not just the addict:

"David, a thirty-five-year old businessman, brought his marriage to the brink of disaster because of his cocaine addiction. At least once or twice a week he would leave home in the evening, supposedly to buy a pack of cigarettes or take a walk, and then not return home or call for two days. His cocaine binges involved marathon sex orgies with prostitutes in fancy hotel rooms. David's wife suspected that his cocaine use involved other women, but she nonetheless covered for him by making excuses to his boss and others to minimize the fallout from his irresponsible and erratic cocaine-induced behavior. She tried everything she knew to get David to stop using cocaine: Blackmail, bribery, suicide threats, calls to the police, even leaving with the kids for a day or two.

She felt inadequate as a wife, believing that if she were sexier, prettier, and more fun-loving David wouldn't be so inclined to use cocaine. She threatened numerous times to leave, file for divorce, and take their two young children with her, but David quickly learned that these were idle threats because she always returned. She kept hoping that he would seek help, but the problem just got worse. She became chronically depressed and felt lonely and isolated. She hated having a part-time husband who didn't seem to care enough about her or their children to stop using cocaine. She finally sought treatment because she felt trapped in an inescapable bind. She loved David and felt sorry for him, but she had to do something to save herself and her children from this horrible mess."

David's addiction took its toll on his family. As we can readily see, his relationship with cocaine took precedence over everything else, which unfortunately included his family. Washton (1990) also says that the addict's accelerating dependence upon cocaine will have a reverberating and potentially deadly effect on the entire family:

But the most profound and damaging effects of cocaine addiction occur silently and insidiously within individual members of the family as they react to the chronic state of crisis and confusion caused by the addict's behavior. These changes are usually subtle at first. But as the cocaine-related problems continue, family members shift their energy and attention more and more away from their own needs, interests, and concerns to the addicts. Family members do this by:

* trying to figure out when the addict is using cocaine.
* reacting to the addict's irrational behavior.
* searching for hidden cocaine supplies.
* pleading and fighting about the addict's unwillingness to seek help.
* covering up for the addict's behavior to employer, friends, and relatives.
* worrying about the addict's whereabouts and health.
* taking care of the addict's financial and legal problems.

Life with an active addict can be a living hell. Africentric values place a high premium on our interconnectedness, and on our need for family unity. With the onset of an individual's dependence upon cocaine, however, we may begin to confuse an unfaltering commitment to the true meaning of those principles with what may actually constitute enabling behaviors on our part.

Africentric imperatives demand that we share one another's pain - this is precisely why it's so hard to separate ourselves from the inevitable decline of the addict. However, misguided attempts to assume what we mistakenly believe to be Africentric efforts at providing love, support, and assistance to the addict infuses the addiction with an absolutely incredible degree of stability and power.

In other words, the addiction continues. As Washton (1990) has accurately observed:

"Addiction cannot flourish without support. If you consciously or unconsciously collude with the addict in refusing to confront or acknowledge the problem, you only further the addiction. Once you quit enabling the addiction, the addict is in trouble because he or she requires a great deal of assistance in maintaining the distorted reality necessary to service his or her addictive needs. Enabling includes a variety of behavior: minimizing, controlling, shielding, taking over responsibilities, and colluding.

*Minimizing is rationalizing, ignoring, or otherwise explaining away the addict's problem and its consequences. It's also saying things like, 'It's not so bad; a lot of people use drugs nowadays,' or 'He's a troubled person. He's had a tough life and needs a chance to work out his problems before he can stop using cocaine.'

*Controlling is attempting to manipulate the addict's cocaine supply and cocaine use. It's also bargaining with the addict to behave, bribing the addict to stop using cocaine, giving the addict ultimatums, or making idle threats.

*Shielding is protecting the addict from the negative consequences of his or her addiction. It's also making excuses, covering up, or otherwise rescuing the addict from trouble.

*Taking over responsibilities includes paying bills or doing any work that should be the addict's responsibility.

*Colluding is helping the addict obtain cocaine or giving the addict cocaine."

A close inspection of the above enabling behaviors reveals that they are far removed from conduct genuinely rooted in Africentric principles. In fact, enabling behaviors can insidiously serve to reinforce the perception within the addict, (and his family) that he is somehow immune from all of the damaging consequences of his addiction. He fails to recognize that the enabling behaviors of those closest to him are sparing him from facing necessary consequences; instead, he foolishly assumes that his own intelligence "saves" him from consequences:

Andre, age 35, began to experiment with crack cocaine after the death of his mother. Married for twelve years and the father of two sons, ages 9 and 5, Andre had led an exemplary life. As president of the local chapter of 100 Black Men, he had helped to develop a number of innovative programs targeted specifically at African American male students in grades K - 4.

He lapsed into a depression after his mother passed. An acquaintance from work promised him that cocaine would provide him with a significant mental boost. This boost would help him to continue in his demanding role as president of the local chapter of 100 Black Men. Andre's wife understandably reacted with alarm to his cocaine use, but she would consistently behave in ways to perpetuate his addiction. She would call in sick for him at work. She even attempted to cancel some of the afterschool programs that Andre had developed for the students. Meanwhile, Andre believed that he was functioning very well - even with his addiction to cocaine.

Interestingly enough, these developments seem to coincide with the emergence of what Martin (1990) defines as, "The Full Flowering of Faith" in the addict. We believe that this process becomes particularly intense whenever the addiction is perpetuated by enabling behaviors. Martin says:

"Suddenly, the addict becomes an expert philosopher. There is no more deep, hidden mystery or secrets of life. The addict has a theory for everything.

Ask him anything on issues within and without the field of his expertise. Not only does he have the answer, but you damn well better agree with him. His is not only an opinion, it's the unarguable truth. I even suspect that a non-exceptional phenomenon takes place here. The disease robs him of his expertise, if he ever had one, and gives him the illusion of authority in all other matters. I further suspect that the disease itself leads the addict down the road of total error. It connects him with the lie of lies. It confirms his suspicion that a successful life requires one to know... better still to know all things."

We can move toward, ultimately embrace, and strategically apply Africentric principles to the dilemma of cocaine dependency among African American men by becoming involved in their programs of rehabilitation and recovery. Our participation in this process would fundamentally consist of the following two measures (Washton, 1990):

1. WE MUST ELIMINATE ALL ENABLING CONDUCT.

We are not suggesting that we shouldn't care. On the contrary, our grounding in the principles of Africentric requires that we demonstrate love all the more and at all costs. The distinguishing characteristic between enabling versus Africentric approaches rests with the enormity of our respect for the latent capabilities of all African American male cocaine addicts. We choose to see beyond the surface to what these men could become via their conscious and deliberate submission to the transforming power of God's grace. Enabling behaviors are essentially non-Africentric in perspective. These behaviors become stagnantly fixated upon the narrow confines of surface appearances. Eventually, hope for the addict is extinguished. We begin to hear statements like: "I don't care; it's not my problem that he became addicted to cocaine" or "Let him pull himself up by his own bootstraps."

2. WE MUST BECOME EDUCATED WITH RESPECT TO THE RELATIONSHIP BETWEEN

family issues, relational patterns, and cocaine dependence. It is critically important that we examine ourselves in order to determine how and in what ways our own behavior feeds into the continuation of the addiction.

Again, we must not confuse enabling behaviors with behaviors that are truly Africentric. The elimination of enabling behaviors among the addict's family members and extended support network necessarily involves the practice of detachment. Detachment seems to go against the grain of Africentric principles and practices. It indicates distance, isolation, and separation. However, the willingness to detach ourselves from the often compelling need to rescue African American men from the consequences of their addiction, i.e., "I had to step in because the system would have conspired to bring him down even further," prevents these men from facing the full consequences of what they're doing. It is precisely when we take the admittedly frightening, yet courageous step of detaching from the addict's behaviors that he may, and we emphasize may, wake up to the reality of God's call for liberation. In *Detachment: Recovery for Family Members* (1987), Reddy and McElfresh address themselves to how the process of detachment works with alcoholics. The process is the same for cocaine:

"For instance, assume that the alcoholic has passed out in his car in the garage. His wife checks on where he is and then leaves him there to spend the night. As understanding of detachment matures, she may still leave him in the car (so that he is aware of his behavior when he awakens), but she would check first to be sure there was no physical condition in need of medical attention and she would probably toss a blanket over him if the weather was cold. The next morning she would quietly describe what happened and why she left him there. 'I wanted you to realize for yourself what you did last night.' This example demonstrates that the alcoholic is allowed to experience the consequences of alcoholism, yet it indicates love and concern for the person."

It is also important to observe that the practice of detachment has a decidedly spiritual quality because we relinquish our enabling control of the addict. Instead, we commit him to the nurturing embrace of God. We give up the often times ego-inflating assumption that we are "saviors". Indeed, there is only one Savior. The emphasis on the spiritual dimension of detachment helps us to maintain our focus on God as the ultimate protector and deliverer.

The spiritual dimensions inherent to the practice of a "consecrated" detachment seems intimately Africentric in nature. We agree with Martin (1990), "Since the disease is spiritual, it is transmitted through a spiritual means - that is a loving relationship with an active addict." Africentricity is fundamentally rooted in a liberating and palpable sense of the spiritual dimension. Africentricity also recognizes that the spiritual dimension weaves itself into the very fabric of life and that its influence is, quite literally, inescapable and complete.

When the family and/or support network of the cocaine dependent African American male decides to detach in ways that are specifically Africentric, they must communicate their rationale for doing so with the addict. This approach preserves the integrity so vital to Africentricity because it conveys to the addict: "We love you enough to explain to you why we have chose to be have toward you in this manner."

It is also important to note that families can aid in the process of recovery for cocaine dependent African American men by virtue of their willingness to step right into the midst of the addict's pain, though not in an enabling way. Then, developments occur within the addict which we can truthfully say will border on the astonishing. God's transforming and empowering presence becomes especially evident because we are helping to carry some of the pain away. Smedes (1978) explains it this way:

"Does love carry people's burdens away? This question still needs to be answered. Can I reduce a neighbor's burden by taking it on myself? The answer is that loving entrance into the pain of another can carry pain away. The experience of pain is a deep mystery. We hardly know what pain is though we have no doubts when we have it. Some of our pain is precisely that of having no burden-carrier in our lives. Consequently, some of the most dramatic relief comes when someone enters our lives and accepts our burdens as his. When persons truly share in their spirit a consciousness of our hurt and loss, and then carry our sorrow, they carry some of it away from us. When love drives a person to share another's pain, the pain becomes less hard to bear. We say this in awe, for it touches one of the deepest mysteries of life."

When we consciously arrive at the courageous decision to share the addict's pain and despair, we can trust that God will help us to distinguish between behaviors which indicate our "loving entrance into pain of another" as opposed to behaviors which enable the addiction to continue. Families would also remain true to the principles of Africentricity by the act of sharing these burdens.

There is yet another dimension to the potentially painful process of eliminating enabling behaviors which typically surround the addict. May (1991) says that we can readily lapse into a state of "addictive helpfulness" whenever we are confronted with the reality of someone's pain and this addictive helpfulness (which, interestingly enough, parallels enabling behaviors) can actually prevent us from offering a truly loving response. May goes on to say:

"It is not easy to just be with the pain of another, to feel it as your own. No wonder we are likely to jump into our habitual responses so quickly. As soon as we start doing something for or to the suffering person, we can minimize the bare agony of feeling that person's pain. It is like that everywhere; our addicted doings act as minor anesthesia."

When we allow ourselves to feel the "bare agony" so painfully evident in the lives of cocaine dependent African American men, we lovingly embrace our Africentric core. Miraculous things begin to happen because we give up the terribly seductive temptation which would have us believe that we can intelligently orchestrate outcomes. Indeed, our decision to eliminate our frenzied helping activities in order that we might genuinely feel this anguish, so poignant, invites God's embrace of the addict and ourselves. God's grace becomes manifest. *Exploring the Road Less Traveled: A Study Guide for Small Groups* (1985), Alice and Walden Howard quote Paul Tillich who authored *The Shaking of the Foundations.*

> "Do you know what it means to be struck by grace? ... We cannot transform our lives, unless we allow them to be transformed by that stroke of grace. It happens or it does not happen. And certainly it does not happen if we try to force it upon ourselves, just as it shall not happen so long as we think, in our self-complacency, that we have no need of it. Grace strikes us when we are in great pain and restlessness. It strikes us when we walk through the dark valley of a meaningless and empty life. It strikes us when we feel that our separation is deeper than usual, because we have violated another life, a life which we loved, or from which we are estranged. It strikes us when our disgust for our own being, our indifference, our weakness, our hostility, and our lack of direction and composure have become intolerable to us. It strikes when, year after year, the longed-for perfection of life does not appear, when the old compulsions reign within us as they have for decades, when despair destroys all joy and courage. Sometimes at that moment, a wave of light breaks into our darkness, and it is as though a voice were saying: "You are accepted. You are accepted, accepted by that which is greater than you, and the name of which you do

133

not know. Do not ask for the name now; perhaps you will find it later. Do not try to do anything now; perhaps later you will do much. Do not seek for anything; do not perform anything; do not intend anything. Simply accept the fact that you are accepted! If that happens to us, we experience grace. After such an experience we may not be better than before, we may not believe more than before. But everything is transformed. In that moment, grace conquers sin, and reconciliation bridges the gulf of estrangement. And nothing is demanded of this experience, no religious or moral or intellectual presupposition, nothing but acceptance... It is such moments that make us love our life, that make us accept ourselves, not in our goodness and self-complacency, but in our certainty of the eternal meaning of our life. We cannot force ourselves to accept ourselves. We cannot compel anyone to accept himself. But sometimes it happens that we receive the power to say "yes" to ourselves, that peace enters into us and makes us whole, that self-hate and self-contempt disappear, and that our self is re-united with itself. Then we can say that grace has come upon us."

God's grace liberates us from the limited perspectives of our addictions. In this excerpt taken from *The Strength to Love,* Martin Luther King Jr., (quoted in Howard, 1985) put it so eloquently:

"Beneath and above the shifting sands of time, the uncertainties that darken our days, and the vicissitudes that cloud our nights is a wise and loving God.

This universe is not a tragic expression of meaningless chaos but a marvelous display of orderly cosmos... Man is not a wisp of smoke from a limitless smoldering, but a child of God created a little lower than the angels.

Above the manyness of time stands the one eternal God, with wisdom to guide us, strength to protect us, and love to keep us.

His boundless love supports and contains us as a mighty ocean contains and supports the tiny drops of every wave. With a surging fullness He is forever moving toward us, seeking to fill the creeks and bays of our lives with unlimited resources."

Another dimension of healing and recovery for cocaine dependent African American men is closely linked with Africentricity.

COMING HOME, AFRICAN STYLE

We have already explored the practical implications arising from the fascinating relationship between Africentric principles, and May's apt description of the homeward call. In closing, we would now like to turn our attention to another dimension to the process of healing and recovery for cocaine dependent African American men that is closely associated with Africentricity and the homeward call.

In 1986, Nicholas C. Cooper-Lewter and Henry H. Mitchell authored a book which has the potential for expanding our views on how we as African Americans achieve and maintain emotional stability. Entitled *Soul Theology: The Heart of Black American Culture*, the primary purpose of the book is to share how we attain emotional balance by virtue of the strengths and weaknesses of our core belief systems about God.

Moreover, Cooper-Lewter and Mitchell have sought to, "retrieve and preserve the rich, life-giving affirmations of the Black oral tradition" as well as to, "clinically validate and offer a pattern of belief and life that heals minds and spirits, helping to prevent pervasive personal and family disintegration."

African American communities convey experiences about the nature of God that helps to sustain us throughout life. For example, "God is able" is a core belief that is richly edifying to us when we're going through a difficult period. In a manner which is so awe-inspiring because of it's

136

intrinsic linkages to the liberating properties of Africentricity and the healing power of the homeward call, Cooper-Lewter and Mitchell have also declared that core beliefs, "are embraced intuitively and emotionally, with or without the ability to express them rationally. Core beliefs are perhaps most authentically expressed when uttered spontaneously in crisis situations."

A lively discussion ensues on how ten core beliefs, still resonant with African American culture, provides us with the inspiration to journey on even in the midst of seemingly insurmountable obstacles. These ten core beliefs are as follows:

* The Providence of God - "And we know that God works in everything for good..." (Romans 8:28)
* The Justice of God - "For whatsoever a man soweth, that he shall also reap." (Galatians 6:7)
* The Majesty and Omnipotence of God - "Hallelujah: for the Lord God omnipotent reigneth!" (Revelation 19:6)
* The Omniscience of God - "Your Father knoweth what things ye have need of, before ye ask." (Matthew 6:8)
* The Goodness of God and Creation - "And God saw everything He had made, and, behold, it was very good." (Genesis 1:31)
* The Grace of God - "For by grace are ye saved and acceptable through faith." (Ephesians 2:8)
* The Equality of Persons - "There is neither Jew nor Greek, there is neither bound nor free, there is neither male nor female; for ye are all one in Christ Jesus." (Galatians 3:28)
* The Uniqueness of Persons: Identity - "Stir up the gift of God which is in thee." (2 Timothy 1:6)

137

* The Family of God and Humanity - "Have we not all one Father?" (Malachi 2:10)
* The Perseverance of Persons - "And let us not be weary in well doing: for in due season we shall reap, if we faint not." (Galatians 6:9)

We have selected one of the case illustrations from Cooper-Lewter and Mitchell's work to demonstrate how these African American core beliefs could be applied to the process of recovery for cocaine dependent African American men. Please note the remarkably practical connections between Africentricity and the homeward call:

"When Harvey, age twenty-nine, came to the clinic, he complained, 'I can't seem to follow through on anything. If this keeps up, I might as well give up.' A professional football player plagued by loneliness and severe depression, Harvey had been taking marijuana and cocaine, and it was starting to interfere with his game. This resulted in a loss of bargaining power, and he was losing his ability to deal with contracts at all. As his emotions soared and plummeted like a roller coaster, he escaped reality and the task of taking responsibility for himself. A small hint from his roommate was all it took to get him to break his escape pattern long enough to visit the clinic.

His complaints poured out easily. 'I lie and escape responsibility.' He even realized he was angry at his mother for deserting him by dying in an auto accident. He had considered killing himself, but he could not follow through on that either, especially since his mother would not have been pleased with him. Since he felt unable to stop life, he decided to change his way of living.

His case history revealed that his father left him and his mother when Harvey was only four. His mother had worked hard to support him, and he was unusually grateful. Meanwhile, she had also been atypically sensitive and permissive about her precious only child's ambition to excel in such rough and dangerous sports like football. Instead of smothering him with over protection, she had joined him in athletic enthusiasm. It all paid off when he made the professional ranks at age twenty-three. He was soon able to support her in leisure. She was delighted, of course, but no more so than he. They became inseparable. 'We were like one person. We were really close. I think I died when she died. I have no desire to go on without her. I can never live life to the fullest without Mother.'

Emotionally speaking, Harvey was still an infant locked in the body of a physical giant. In his most lucid and trusting moments, he confessed needs of what can best be expressed as cuddling in his mother's arms. The women he liked were prone to be well-endowed like his mother, even though he called them 'girls.' He was convinced that none of them was 'woman enough to replace Mom.' All 240 pounds of this giant belonged to a mother whom he refused to allow to die. He had to keep her because of the self-imposed limit placed on what he could expect and accept from other women. He had already stopped the clock of his emotional life prior to his mother's death. He was still her husband/protector and her gladiator/son.

However, this fantasy role was not stable. At one moment he would be, as he said, angry at his mother for abandoning him. Then he would feel guilty and do things that the therapist recognized as self-punishment. Depression associated with his guilt were attempts to share the death state with his mother. They also served the purpose of checking the anger he himself could sense as dangerous. In a way, he had already accepted death rather than to try to control himself and live without his mother.

The therapy prescribed for Harvey moved through five aspects. First, he was encouraged to release, understand and finally to handle his feelings of stress. This allowed him to deal with them without the use of drugs or escapes into fantasy. Then he was assisted in sorting out his own identity, instead of having the previous symbiotic existence with his mother. Thirdly, he was given mental and behavioral exercises affirming the newborn person he was becoming. The fourth step was to help him visualize his new, emerging identity. Then finally, using the discipline and perseverance associated with football practice, he was able to maintain determination to apply all this to handling real life.

Harvey's response to this process was as stormy as his unstable emotional life. Every time he began to accept his mother's death, he would displace his anger onto the therapist. Then he would return to reality, feel guilty, and escape the therapist at the next appointment. Later on, as he made real progress, he would fear to go further and miss appointments. He was not anxious to grow up, because he was not at all sure that he could handle that level of mature responsibility.

The therapist recorded a tape for Harvey and instructed him to listen to it on a regular basis. It contained some of his mother's favorite religious songs, and they supported the growth he needed with familiar phrases that reached deep within his psyche. For instance, the song "Precious Lord, Take My Hand" affirmed Harvey's present dependency, but it moved on to say, "let me stand" which spoke right to his area of need. Another song prayed, "Lord, Help Me to Hold Out." It said what he wanted to say and strengthened his determination, without his having to put it in pious-sounding words. This was important, because he was afraid to look or sound as deeply religious as he was becoming.

Harvey had not earlier been able to reduce his dependence on drugs, but he now found that mental and spiritual training were very effective aids in reducing even his desire for drugs. As he concluded his sessions, he knew that his mother would have been proud of the way he was progressing off the drugs and his new tastes in music and reading materials."

This case shows us that Harvey learned to embrace the need to live Africentrically. This means that he came back to the systems of core beliefs so integral to the maintenance of our health and wellness as vibrant African American men. Of course, this also means that he accepted the homeward call which had been blindly masked by his dependence upon drugs. Thus, he came home to rest in God's loving embrace.

Practical implications for substance abuse treatment centers would include a strong and vivid emphasis on the development of a treatment community which replicates a West African frame of reference in terms of program design, philosophy, and operations. For example, the value of interdependence among patients would be encouraged and promoted in order to enhance prospects for the recovery of everyone.

Individualism would be discouraged because of its tendency to fragment or detract from the beginning of a true healing journey. Bethel A.M.E. Church in Baltimore, Maryland (pastored by Rev. Frank M. Reid III) has pioneered an approach to the delivery from substance abuse problems among African Americans. This congregation recognizes that a healthy reliance upon spiritual dimensions is the pivotal ingredient to healing and recovery.

Entitled "Freedom Now Ministry: Jesus Is Your Victory" Bethel's program is founded upon the following twelve principles, all gleaned from the timeless truths of what makes Alcoholics Anonymous so effective:

12 WAYS TO VICTORY OVER ALCOHOL AND DRUG ABUSE

1. Recognize that you must stop drinking and using drugs and acknowledge and accept that you cannot control using alcohol or drugs on your own or in your own power. Scriptures: Romans 3:23, Matthew 6:33, John 3:16 and I Timothy 2:1-5.

2. Learn to believe that God can and will help you live a sober lifestyle through Jesus Christ. Scriptures: Ephesians 1:21, Philippians 2:9, Romans 10:13-17, Acts 1:9, II Timothy 1:7 and Joel 2:25.

3. Make a quality decision to let God have complete control over your life through the dictates of His Word. Matthew 6:24-34, I Peter 5:7, John 10:27-29, John 4:13-14, and Isaiah 54:17.

4. Mentally examine yourself and on paper, list ways you can change your behavioral pattern. Psalm 139:23-24 and I Corinthians 11:28.

5. Pray to God in the name of Jesus and ask Him to give you the strength to help you correct your wrongs and not be ashamed to confess your faults to others. Psalm 51:3, I John 3:8, Psalm 32:5, James 5:16, and II Timothy 3:16.

6. Thank God and praise Him for helping you remove these challenges. Nehemiah 9:15-17, Isaiah 6:6-7, Psalm 10:2-3, and II Corinthians 5:17.

7. Humble yourself before God and thank Him for His mercy and for giving you the strength to overcome your faults. John 16:23-24, Luke 11:9-10, James 4:10, I Peter 5:5-6, and Psalm 10:57.

8. Write down all those you have harmed and prepare yourself to make restitution. Luke 19:1, Matthew 5:23-24, and Acts 9:1-5.

9. Make restitution when possible without hurting others. Luke 15:11-32 and Ephesians 5:15-18.

10. Examine yourself on a daily basis to see if you are being a doer of the Word and not just a hearer only. James 1:22, Psalm 38:18, and II Corinthians 7:9-10.

11. Continue to pray and give thanks to God for helping you to grow in knowledge of Him and the strength to act on his Word. Luke 18:1, Joshua 1:8, Psalm 1:1-3, and II Timothy 2:1-5, and I Thessalonians 5:18.

12. Once you have achieved victory over alcohol and drugs, do not return to using, but share your testimony with those who are suffering from alcohol and/or drug abuse and continue to do the Word. Mark 16:15, Acts 1:8, and Matthew 10:8.

SUPPLEMENTAL SCRIPTURES
Titus 1:2, Hebrews 6:18, Matthew 11:28, John 12:24, Psalm 31:23-24, John 6:31-32, James 1:26, and II Timothy 4:13.

Nothing but the blood of Jesus . . .

Conclusion

Cocaine has wreaked havoc in the lives of so many African American men that it is imperative that we take another look at the solutions currently available in society and see where improvement can be made. Within this context, we find one readily workable solution that has been utilized throughout the ages namely, an Africentrist perspective grounded in spiritual values and principles.

Rather than abandoning African American addicts to the prevailing systems in place, it is necessary that we surround them with the nurturing families and kinship groups to the best of our abilities. It is evident that the impact on families has been devastating, in terms of loss of manpower due to death and incarceration, the stress imposed upon the family group and the society having such a burden. The chaos in our lives will remain unless we implement some other programs that could prove to be more effective.

The current paradigms of psychological stratagems presently utilized have, we must admit failed miserably in their efforts to rehabilitate. The rate of relapse exceeds 85% in this nation and unless we look to another principle, a higher principle and attempt to transcend this problem, the deterioration of our families, drug abuse related criminal behavior, and death will only continue to occur.

We have weathered storms too numerous to mention, and still, our God has not abandoned us, nor will He ever do so. A return to our true heritage as a strong and culturally vibrant African American people can help us to heal.

One of the most interesting aspects of the proposed solutions would be a return to an Africentric perspective. Evidence of the interplay between melanin and co-polymerization in the brain structure that contributes to an accelerated and prolonged reaction in African Americans seems to require further research. Out of that research may come a more effective treatment in terms of detoxification, so there is hope on the horizons, if we bravely face the challenges before us.

We should not neglect or ignore the subtle evidence of racism in our communities from the alcohol industry and stand up to the institutions that seek to promote an addictive personality in our children and their subsequent ensnarement in an addiction that could kill them. The price of our neglect is too high to pay. Can we continue to do this and ignore the surmounting evidence that there are problems that require our immediate attention?

It would seem that cocaine dependent African American men who are engaged in an evolving process of recovery are uniquely endowed by God to teach us significant truths about ourselves. An addict may gradually learn to lean on the everlasting arms of God. But, I also propose that the addict is not alone. There are support groups available and we, ourselves, need to evolve. That evolution can take place in our churches, informal meetings, family conferences and school discussions. We cannot isolate ourselves from each other. Rather, we must embrace each other. Within this caring embrace, we will win, we will survive, and we will have learned something beneficial through our struggle. Freedom from addiction is not only physical but an emergence of the personality from that of self-hatred and self-indulgence which is pervasive in American society as a whole to a more wholistic/spiritual approach to life.

The foundation of African cultures has always been spiritual with the family and community group working together to monitor the behavior of its members, to encourage meaningful existence that can benefit the group and to strongly censor conduct that is destructive. We must stop turning an apathetic ear and indifferent eye to others who need our help.

Let us not abandon centuries of culture since we were dispossessed of our homeland but again, incorporate structures and values into our daily lives that can only help us to emerge free of all the shackles that are around us-namely, poverty, addiction, crime, hopelessness and despair. By embracing these values, a deep abiding spiritual objective, a replacement of a materialistic/individualistic ethical system with a spiritual/collective system, a positive result should invariably occur.

REFERENCES

Akbar, N. (1991). *Visions for Black Men.* Nashville, TN: Winston-Derek Publishers.

Asante, M.K. (1991). *Afrocentricity.* Trenton, NJ: Africa World Press.

Bell, P. (1990). *Chemical Dependency and the African-American: Counseling Strategies and Community Issues.* Century City, MN: Hazelden.

Billingsley, A. (1968). *Black Families in White America,* Englewood Cliffs, NJ: Prentice-Hall.

Boskin, J. (1986). *Sambo: The Rise and Demise of an American Court Jester.* New York: Oxford University Press.

Boyd-Franklin, N. (1989). *Black Families in Therapy: Multisystems Approach.* New York: Guilford Press.

Brisbane, F. and M. Womble. (1987). *Treatment of Black Alcoholics.* New York: Sage Press.

Cannon, M. and B. Locke. (1977). "Being Black May Be Detrimental to One's Health: Myth or Reality?" *Phylon,* Vol. 33, pp 408-428.

Cazenave, N.A. (1981). "Black Men in America: The Quest for `Manhood'. In H.P. McAdoo (Ed.), *Black Families,* pp 176-186. Beverly Hills, CA: Sage Press.

Chilman, N.C. (1966). *Growing up Poor.* Washington. D.C.: U.S. Department of Health, Education, and Welfare.

Cole, L. (1989). *Never Too Young to Die: The Death of Len Bias.* New York: Pantheon Books.

Davis, G. and G.Watson. (1985). *Black Life in Corporate America: Swimming in the Mainstream* New York: Anchor Books.

Davis, O. (1969). "Our Shining Black Prince" in *Malcolm X: The Man and His Times,* edited by John Henrik Clarke. New York: MacMillan.

Drake, S. & H. Cayton. (1945). *Black Metropolis.* New York: Harcourt/Brace.

Ellison, R. (1980). *Invisible Man.* New York: Signet Books.

Flowers, R. (1988). *Minorities & Criminality.* New York: Greenwood Press.

Foster, M. and L. Perry. (1982) "*Self-Valuation Among Blacks.*" *Social Work,* pp 61-66. Silver Spring, MD: National Association of Social Workers

Frazier, E.F. (1932). *The Negro Family in Chicago.* Chicago: University of Chicago Press.

Frazier, E.F. (1939) *The Negro Family in the United States,* Chicago: University of Chicago Press.

Gary, L.E. (Eds.) (1981). *Black Men.* Beverly Hills, CA: Sage Press.

Gary, L.E. (Ed.) (1978). *Mental Health: A Challenge to the Black Community.* Philadelphia: Dorrace.

Gary, L.E., and B.R. Leashore. (1982). "High-Risk Status of Black Men." *Social Work,* 45-54. Silver Spring, MD: National Association of Social Workers.

Gary, L.E., B. Leashore, C. Howard, and Buckner-Dowell. (1987) *Help-Seeking Behavior Among Black Males.* Washington, D.C.: Howard University Institute for Urban Affairs and Research.

Gary, L.E. (1985). *Depressive Symptomatology Among Black Men.* Winter, Vol. 21: No. 4. Washington D.C.: Howard University Institute for Urban Affairs and Research.

Georges-Abeyie, D. (1984). *The Criminal Justice System and Blacks.* New York: Clark Roardman.

Grier, W.H. and P.M. Cobbs. (1968). *Black Rage.* San Francisco: Harper Torchbooks.

Gutman, H.G. (1976). *The Black Family in Slavery and Freedom:* 1750-1925. New York: Vintage Books.

Hacker, G., R. Collins, and M. Jacobson. (1987). *Marketing Booze to Blacks.* Washington, D.C: The Center for Science in the Public Interest.

Hare, N., Ph.D. and J. Hare, Ed.D (Eds). (1989). *Crisis in Black Sexual Politics.* San Francisco: Black Think Tank.

Harper, F. (Ed.) (1976). *Alcohol Abuse and Black America.* Virginia: Douglas Publishers.

Hendricks, L., S. Ceasar, and L. Gary. (Eds.). (1987) (in press) *Issues in Racial and Comparative Research.* Washington, D.C.: Howard University Institute for Urban Affairs Research.

Herskovits, M.J. (1935). "Social History of the Negro." In C. Murchinson (Ed.), *A Handbook of Social Psychology.* Worcester, MA: Clark University Press, pp. 207-267.

Hill, P. (1992). *Coming of Age: African American Male Rites of Passage.* Chicago: African American Images.

Hill, R. (1971). *The Strengths of Black Families.* New York: Emerson Hall.

Howard, A. and W. Howard. (1985). *Exploring the Road Less Traveled: A Study Guide for Small Groups.* New York: Simon and Schuster.

Howard University Institute for Urban Affairs and Research. (1986). *Strong Black Families: Research Findings,* Vol. 11, No. 1. Washington, D.C.

Jones, B.E., G. Beverly, and J. Jospitre (1982). "Survey of Psychotherapy with Black Men." *American Journal of Psychiatry,* Vol. 139: pp 1174-1177.

King, R., M.D. (1990). *African Origins of Biological Psychiatry.* Germantown, TN: Seymour-Smith.

Kessler, R.C., R.H. Price, and C.B. Wortman. (1985). "Social Factors in Psychopathology: Stress, Social Support and Coping Processes." *Annual Review of Psychology,* Vol. 31: pp 531-572.

Kunjufu, J. (1990). *Countering the Conspiracy to Destroy Black Boys,* Volume 3. Chicago: African American Images.

Liebow, E. (1967). *Tally's Corner: A Study of Street Corner Men.* Boston: Brown Publishing.

"Losing Ground." (April 6, 1992). *Newsweek.* Vol. 119: No. 7

Ludwig, A., A. Winkle, and L. Stark. (1974). "The First Drink: Psychological Aspects of Craving." *Archives of General Psychiatry.* Vol. 30: pp 539-547.

Majors, R. and J. Billson. (1992). *Cool Pose: The Dilemmas of Black Manhood in America.* New York: Lexington Books.

Martin, J.A. (1990). *Blessed are the Addicts: The Spiritual Side Of Alcoholism, Addiction, and Recovery.* New York: Harper Collins.

Martin, J., and E. Martin. (1985). *The Helping Tradition in the Black Family and Community.* Silver Spring, MD: National Association of Social Workers.

May, G. (1988). *Addiction and Grace: Love and Spirituality in the Healing Of Addictions*. San Francisco: Harper Collins.

May, G. (1991). *The Awakened Heart: Living Beyond Addiction*. San Francisco: Harper Collins.

Mays, V. (1985). "The Black American and Psychotherapy: The Dilemma", *Psychotherapy*, 22, 379-388.

Milburn, N.G., et.al., (1984)."Depressive Symptoms and Social Network Characteristics." Paper presented at the National Association of Social Workers Health Conference, Washington, DC.

Miller, W. (1958). "Lower-Class Culture as a Generating Milieu of Gang Delinquency." *Journal of Social Issues*, Vol. 14: pp 5-19.

Minsky, T. (February 23, 1984). "The Odds on Being Slain-Worse for Young Black Males." *Boston Globe*, pp 1, 47.

Mitchell, H.H., and N.C. Lewter. (1986). *Soul Theology: The Heart of Black American Culture*. San Francisco: Harper and Row.

Neighbors, H. W., J.S. Jackson, P.J. Bowman, and G. Gurin.(1983). *Stress, Coping, and Black Mental Health. Journal of Prevention in Human Service*, pp 2, 5-29.

Nobles, W., Ph.D, and L. Goddard, Ph.D.(1989). "Drugs in the African-American Community: A Clear and Present Danger." New York: National Urban League.

Nobles, W., L. Goddard, and W. Cavil. (1985). *The KM EBIT HUSIA: Authoritative Utterances of Exceptional Insight for the Black Family.* Oakland, CA: Black Family Institute Publication.

Nobles, Goddard, Cavil, and George. (1987). The *Culture of Drugs in the Black Community.* Oakland, CA: Black Family Institute Publication.

Primm, B. J. (1987). "Drug Use: Special Implications for Black America." *The State of Black America.* New York: National Urban League.

Reddy, B. and O. McElfresh (1987). *Detachment: Recovery for Family Members.* Park Ridge, IL: Parkside Medical Services.

Scanzoni, J. (1970). *The Black Family in Modern Society.* Boston: Alyn and Beachum.

Schmoke, K. L. (April, 1989) "First Word." *Omni,* Vol. 11, No. 7.

Smedes, L. (1978). *Love Within Limits: A Realist's View of I Corinthians 13.* Grand Rapids, MI: William B. Eerdmans Publishing Company.

"Speaking Out: What Must Be Done." *Ebony* (August, 1989), Vol. 44:No:10.

Stack, C.B. (1974). *All Our Kin: Strategies for Survival in the Black Community.* New York: Harper and Row.

Staples, R. (1982). *Black* Masculinity: *The Black Man's Role in American Society.* San Francisco: Black Scholar Press.

Stewart, J., and J. Scott. (1978). "The Institutional Decimation of the Black American Male." *Western Journal of Black Studies*, pp 2, 82-93.

Swan, A. (1989) "Families of Imprisoned Black Men." In *Crisis In Black Sexual Politics*, edited by Hare, N., Ph.D., and Hare, J., Ed.D. San Francisco: Black Think Tank.

Thomas, A. and S. Sillen. *Racism and Psychiatry.* (1972). New York: Brunner/Mazel.

"A Tide of Drug Killing." (January 16, 1989). *Newsweek.* Vol. 113, No 3.

Tinney, J.S. (1981). "The Religious Experience of Black Men." In L.E. Gary (Ed.), *Black Men*, 269-276. Beverly Hills, CA: Sage Press.

Vista Hill Foundation. (March, 1987). *Drug Abuse and Alcoholism Newsletter.* Vol. XVI, No. 3., San Diego: Vista Hill Foundation.

Wallace, J. (1985). *Alcoholism: New Light on the Disease,* Newport, RI: Edgehill Publications.

Walton, H.W. (1985). *Invisible politics: Black Political Behavior.* Albany, NY: State University of New York Press.

"The War on Crack: Who's the Real Enemy?" (November/December 1990). *The Family Therapy Networker.*

Washton, A. (1989) *Cocaine Addiction: Treatment, Recovery, and Relapse Prevention,* New York: W.W. Norton.

Watts, T.D., and R. Wright (Eds.). (1989) *Alcoholism in Minority Populations.* Springfield, IL: Thomas Publishing.

Whitfield, C. (1989). *Healing the Child Within.* Deerfield Beach, FL: Heath Communications.

"Why Do Blacks Die Young?" (September 16, 1991). *Time,* Vol. 138: No. 11.

Wilkinson, D., and R. Taylor. (1977). *The Black Male in America.* Chicago, IL: Nelson-Hill.

Willie, C. (1970). *The Family Life of the Black Family.* Columbus, OH: Charles E. Merrill Books

Wilson, A. (1981). "The Psychological Development of the Black Child." *Black Books Bulletin,* Vol. 7, No. 2.

Wright, B. (1984). *The Psychopathic Racial Personality and Other Essays.* Chicago, IL: Third World Press.